How to Make Custom-Fit
Bras & Lingerie

Also by Don McCunn

Paper

How to Make Sewing Patterns

website: How-to-Make-Sewing-Patterns.com

E-Books: Text Only

An Introduction to Pattern Design

website: Pattern-Design-Guides.com

E-Books: Interactive

How to Make Bikinis and Bandeaux

How to Make Bust Sling Bras

How to Make Custom-Fit Bras

How to Make Custom-Fit Slopers

How to Make A Custom Dress Form

How to Make Custom-Fit Corsets

Interactive e-Books include
embedded demonstration videos
website: Pattern-Design-Guides.com

Patterns for Fashion Dolls

website: Patterns-for-Fashion-Dolls.com

How to Make Custom-Fit
Bras & Lingerie

Don McCunn

Design Enterprises of San Francisco

Dedication

For my students both in the classroom and in my online classes
whose questions and enthusiasm have kept me going and led me forward.

For my models who have made my
ongoing research and development possible.

And for my wife whose continued support has
made all my endeavors possible.

Library of Congress Control Number: 2017900652

Hardback Edition ISBN: 978-0-932538-38-3
Paperback Edition ISBN: 978-0-932538-39-0

Publisher's Cataloging-in-Publication
(Provided by Quality Books, Inc.)

McCunn, Donald H., author.
How to make custom-fit bras & lingerie / Don McCunn.
pages cm
Includes index.
LCCN 2017900652
ISBN-13: 978-0-932538-38-3 (hardback)
ISBN-10: 0-932538-38-X (hardback)
ISBN-13: 978-0-932538-39-0 (paperback)
ISBN-10: 0-932538-39-8 (paperback)

1. Brassieres. 2. Lingerie. I. Title. II. Title:
How to make custom-fit bras and lingerie.

TT670.M43 2017   646.4'204
                        QBI17-824

DESIGN ENTERPRISES OF SAN FRANCISCO
1007 Castro Street, San Francisco, CA 94114
Websites: deofsf.com & How-to-Make-Custom-Fit-Bras.com

Available to the trade from Ingram Book Company

Acknowledgments

When I began teaching pattern design to adults at a local college in the 1970s, I was asked, "How do you make a pattern for a bra?" At the time, I was deeply immersed in working out techniques for outerwear. Finding the appropriate supplies for making bras seemed like a difficult if not impossible task.

After the advent of the Internet, I was again asked this question during an author chat. Realizing the resources for making bras had become more readily available, I started investigating how to make custom-fit patterns for bras.

In addition to supplies and techniques, I needed fitting/photo models willing to help me test concepts. And, over the years, I have been inspired by models with positive attitudes about how the work we were doing would benefit women requiring this type of support.

I have also been very fortunate in having women in my online classes who have been very helpful in talking me through the diverse issues they have experienced with bras. Their penetrating questions and application of my techniques to a wide variety of figure shapes has led me to invaluable discoveries not the least of which is using Glad's Press'n Seal for making supportive and accurate molds for the patterns in this book.

I would like to extend a special thanks to Susan Stacy of FabricDepotCo.com for sharing her expert knowledge about fabrics and supplies for making bras, lingerie, and swimwear.

Finally, everything I do is because of the incredible support I receive from my wife Roxey.

Table of Contents

Introduction

A well-fitted bra is a challenge for many women. Outer garments are designed to cover the body without restricting movement, so they need to either have some stretch or be slightly loose fitting. Bras, on the other hand, may need to provide support as well as coverage. To minimize the movement of breast tissue, they must fit closely. Yet, for breathing, they must also allow for expansion of the rib cage.

This book shows how to address these issues in creating custom-fit patterns for a variety of bra styles: bikini, bandeau, athletic, bust-sling, conventional, and athletic. The approach you choose depends on the body being covered, the function of the garment, and the style desired. Other factors to consider are the time you have available and your sewing experience. The examples in this book start from the easiest and quickest patterns to make, then proceed to the more involved. This book also shows how to create custom-fit patterns for bikini bottoms and fitted briefs.

When making bras for yourself, the fitting process is easier when there is someone to help you. This fitting buddy does not need to know how to sew but should be willing to take whatever time is necessary to fit you correctly. Instructions are also included for how you can do it yourself (DIY).

While the primary goal of this book is to show how to create custom-fit bras and lingerie, the resulting patterns do not need to be limited to creating undergarments. They can be used to create two-piece swimsuits, tops, dresses, and gowns. Sewing instructions are included for diverse examples.

Bikini Bra

Bandeau Bra

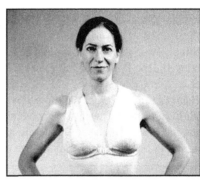
Bust-Sling Bra

Conventional Bra

Lingerie

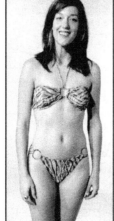
Swimsuit

Bust-Sling Dress

Bandeau Gown

Materials and Supplies

The specific materials and findings you will need depend on the style of garment you are making. There is no limitation on the fashion fabric you use. For custom-fit bras and tops, however, woven fabric should be used to provide the necessary support; knit fabric should be lined with non-stretch fabric.

Basic Materials
Some basic materials you will need include the following:

- Pattern Paper
- Muslin
- Bias Tape
- Velcro
- Glad's Press'n Seal (for some fitting techniques)
- Masking Tape (for some fitting techniques)
- Poster Board
- 1/4" (6 mm) Elastic (Chlorine and Salt Water resistant for swimsuits.)
- 3/4" (18 mm) Elastic (Chlorine and Salt Water resistant for swimsuits.)
- Cording (Shoe laces are great for trial garments.)
- Fashion Fabric

Glad's Press'n Seal

Materials for Conventional Bras
Conventional bras require very specific supplies which are described in more detail on page 112. Some of these, such as bra strap elastic, rings, and sliders are used for a variety of projects described in this book. There are three different types of elastic used for bras. Each one has an external, visible, fashion fabric side and a softer, plush side next to the skin.

- Bra Strap Elastic tends to have plain edges so it will slide easily through the adjusting sliders. It is important to use the same size for the Bra Strap and the Slider.
- Bra Band Elastic is used at the top and bottom of the Bra Band to control the overall fit of the bra. The elastic for the top is usually smaller than the elastic on the bottom. Bra Band elastic frequently has one decorative picot edge.
- Neckline Elastic is decorative along one edge. It comes in many different styles.

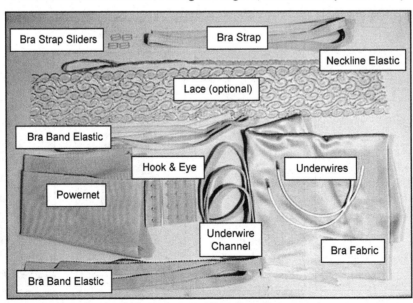

Conventional Bra Supplies

Bikini Tops

The Bikini Bra does not provide as much support as the Bust Sling or Conventional Bra so works best for women with small to medium cup sizes. There are three basic ways a Bikini Top can be shaped: with gathers, a dart, or a princess seam. The Bikini Bra can be tied around the neck with a second tie around the rib cage. Or, tension on the neck can be avoided by using straps in a "X" across the back. The Bikini Bra can also have a front opening clasp.

| Neck Ties | "X" Back | Font Opening Clasp |

The primary differences between a Bikini Bra and a Bikini Swimsuit Top are material and finishing techniques, so the same pattern can be used. To use the Bikini Top pattern for dresses and lingerie as well as a more modest Swimsuit Top, see the instructions for adding a "skirt" starting on page 27.

The Pattern Design Process

For the Basic Bikini Top, use Velcro, bias tape, and bra strap sliders to determine the design lines directly on the body. These design lines can then be used to create the pattern.

1. Create the design lines using Velcro, bias tape, and bra strap sliders.
2. Measure where the design lines are located on the body.
3. Use the measurements to draw the pattern.
4. To verify the design is the look desired, cut the pattern out of scrap fabric and sew the Bikini Top.

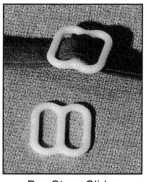

Bra Strap Slider

Creating the Basic Bikini Top Pattern

I. Create the Shape for the Bikini Top

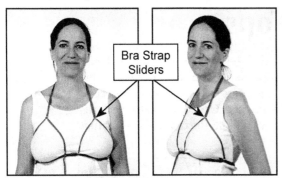

The Design Lines of the Bikini Top

1. Secure Velcro around the rib cage.
2. Secure a length of bias tape to the Velcro at Center Front.
3. Secure a second length of bias tape to the Velcro at the side of the breast.
4. Thread both bias tapes through two bra strap sliders.
5. Wrap the two bias tapes behind the neck and secure them to the Velcro on the other side of the body.
6. Adjust the positions of the sliders and bias tapes to create the shape desired for the Bikini Top.

II. Measure then Draw the Bikini Top

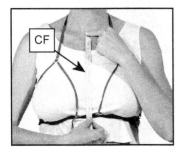
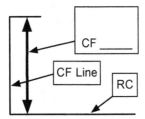

1. Measure down Center Front from the base of the neck to the top of the Velcro at the rib cage and record as CF.
2. Draw a vertical line that is the CF length. This is the Center Front, CF, line.
3. At the top of this vertical line, draw a horizontal line for the location of the neck.
4. At the bottom of this vertical line, draw a second line at right angles to it. This is the Rib Cage, RC, line. The length of the Rib Cage line is not important at this time.

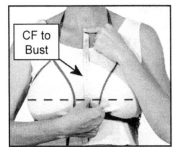
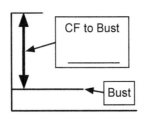

5. Measure down the Center Front from the base of the neck to the fullest part of the bust.
6. On the pattern, measure down on the CF line the CF to Bust length and make a mark.
7. Draw a line at right angles to the Center Front line at this mark. This is the Bust line.

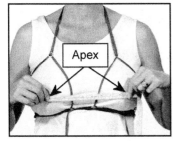
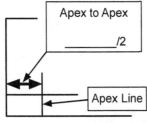

8. Measure across the bust from Apex to Apex.
9. On the pattern, measure out from CF 1/2 the Apex to Apex measurement and make a mark on the Bust line.
10. Draw a line parallel to Center Front through this mark. This is the Apex line.

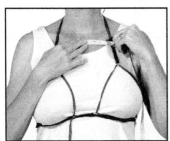
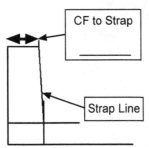

11. Measure out from Center Front to the bias tape representing the Bikini strap.
12. Mark this location on the pattern.
13. Draw a line from this mark to the Apex of the Bust. This is the Strap line of the Bikini.

II. Measure then Draw the Bikini Top, cont'd

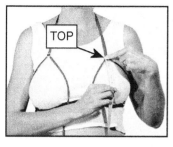

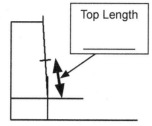

Top Length

_____

14. Measure from the top of the Bikini triangle to the Apex of the bust.
15. Mark this length on the Strap line created in Step 13.

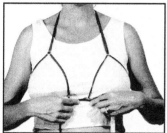

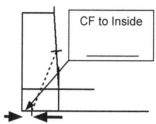

CF to Inside

_____

16. Measure out from Center Front to the bias tape at the rib cage. If there is to be no separation between the two Bikini triangles, this will be 0" (zero).
17. Mark this length on the Rib Cage line.
18. Draw a dotted line from the top of the Bikini to this mark on the Rib Cage.

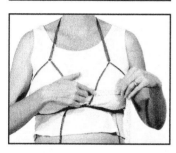

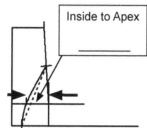

Inside to Apex

_____

19. At the full Bust level, measure from the bias tape to the Apex of the Bust.
20. Mark this length on the Bust line.
21. Draw a curved line from the top of the Bikini down to the Rib Cage. This is the inside seam of the Bikini Top.

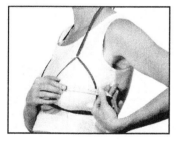

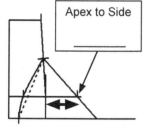

Apex to Side

_____

22. Measure from the Apex of the Bust to the side of the Bikini triangle.
23. Mark this length on the Bust line.
24. Draw a line from the top of Bikini through this mark and down to the Rib Cage line. This is the outside seam of the Bikini Top.

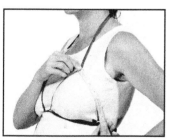

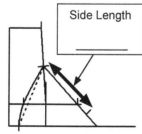

Side Length

_____

25. Measure the side of the Bikini's length from the top to the rib cage.
26. Mark this length on the outside seam of the Bikini Top.

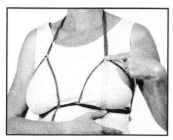

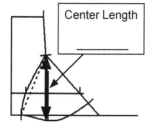

Center Length

_____

27. Measure the length of the Bikini from the top to the Rib Cage over the Apex.
28. Extend the Apex center line to this length.
29. Draw a curved line from the inside seam of the Bikini, to the bottom of the Apex center line, then up to the outside of the Bikini established in Step 26.

This completes the basic pattern shape.

Sewing a Trial Bikini Top

I. Add Casing & Seam Allowances

The instructions below show how to add a ring to the top and a casing for cording at the rib cage to verify the fit.

1. Add 1/4" (6 mm) seam allowance along the two sides of the Bikini.
2. Draw a horizontal line 1/2" (12 mm) down from the top of the Bikini for the ring and add a 3/4" (18 mm) seam allowance.
3. To draw the sides of the seam allowance, fold along the line for the ring.
4. Add a casing allowance along the bottom curve of the Bikini. This should be slightly wider than the cord you are using.
5. Add a seam allowance at the bottom that is the height of the casing plus 1/2" (12 mm).
6. Cut 2 Bikini Tops out of fabric. If you are using stretch fabric, the direction of greatest stretch should be around the body.

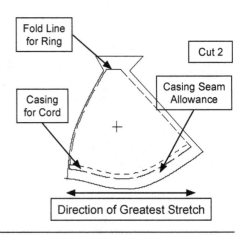

II. Sew the Bikini Top

To stabilize the sides of the Bikini Top, sew 1/4" (6 mm) elastic along the edges. When you are sewing elastic, use 100% polyester thread and ballpoint needles in your sewing machine. These instructions show how to make a trial Bikini Top out of muslin.

1. Cut 1/4" (6 mm) elastic for the two sides of each Bikini triangle. The elastic should be slightly smaller than the distance from the fold line for the ring at the top and the casing line for the cord at the bottom.
2. Pin the elastic on the wrong side of the fabric, then use a 3 mm zigzag to sew the elastic to the muslin.
3. Turn the elastic to the inside of the Bikini and zigzag in place.
4. Thread a 3/4" (18 mm) ring through the top of the Bikini, then topstitch the ring in place with a small 1 mm zigzag stitch.
5. Cut cording that is the circumference of the rib cage plus 24" (60 cm) for ties.
6. Turn the bottom seam allowance for the cord casing to the inside of the Bikini with the cord inside, then hand baste the casing in place.
7. Use a 1 mm wide zigzag to sew the cord casing. If you use a zipper or hem foot, it will help hold the cord in place. If you use a zipper foot, verify that it will accommodate a 1 mm wide zigzag.
8. Trim the top and bottom seam allowances close to the zigzag stitching.
9. Cut two cords for the Bikini straps that are 24" (60 cm) long and tie to the top of the rings.
10. Do a trial fitting of the Bikini Top.

Qty	Materials
1 yd	1/4" (6 mm) Elastic
2	3/4" (20 mm) Rings
1	Fashion Fabric for top
3 yds	Cording (or shoe laces)

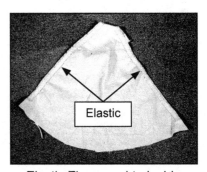

Elastic Zigzagged to Inside

Trial Bikini Top

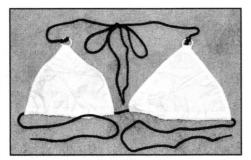

Finished Bikini Top

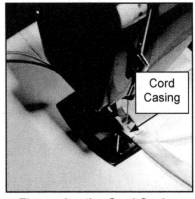

Zigzagging the Cord Casing

14

Adding a Dart to a Bikini Top

There are two ways to add a dart to a Bikini Top.
- Drape a dart, as shown below, while taking the initial measurements and before removing the bias tape and Velcro.
- Add a dart to an existing Bikini Top pattern during a second fitting. See steps I through III below.

Drape a Dart During Measurements

 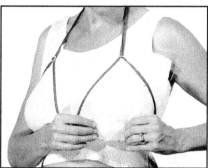 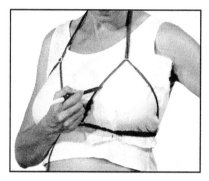

1. From the Apex, slash a square of muslin down to the rib cage.
2. Fit it under the bias tape and Velcro overlapping for the dart.

3. Place masking tape to hold the dart closed.

4. Draw in the edges of the bikini design.
5. Remove the muslin and trace the muslin for the pattern.
6. Proceed to Step III.

I. Prepare Muslin from a Bikini Top Pattern

To add a dart to an existing Bikini Top pattern, use muslin or other scrap fabric for a fitting. Some women may have one breast larger than the other. Make the pattern for the larger breast. The resulting pattern can be used to add an optional foam Underlining.

1. Cut the Bikini Top pattern from page 14 out of muslin.
2. From the bottom of the muslin, cut a slash in the fabric straight up to the Apex of the bust. This will be the dart line.
3. Stay stitch the sides and bottom of the muslin along the sewing lines.
4. Press the side seam allowances under and topstitch in place.
5. Pin the center of a length of bias tape along the bottom of the muslin between the Center Front and the cut for the dart, then zigzag in place.
6. Pin the center of a second length of bias tape between the cut for the dart and the side of the muslin, then zigzag in place.
7. Thread the top of the muslin through a plastic ring, then topstitch in place.

Qty	Materials
1	12" (30 cm) Square of Muslin
1	3/4" (20 mm) Plastic Ring
3	48" (1.25 m) of Bias Tape
1	36" (1 m) of Velcro

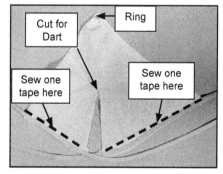

Muslin Bikini Top

II. Fit the Muslin

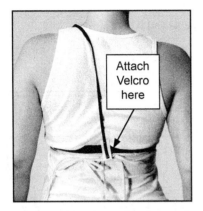
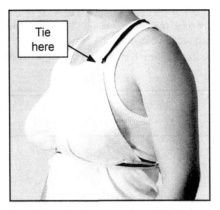
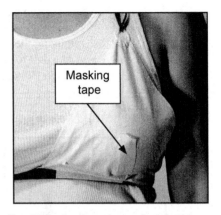

1. Sew a short piece of Velcro to the end of the back bias tape.
2. Attach the Velcro from step 1 to the center of the long Velcro around the rib cage.
3. Attach the long Velcro around the rib cage just below the bust.
4. Loop the bias tape from Center Back through the plastic ring at the top of the bikini and tie it in place.
5. Tie the bias tapes on the bottom of the Bikini around the rib cage.
6. Adjust the size of the dart by shifting the rib cage bias until the desired fit is achieved.
7. Tape the dart shape closed with masking tape.
8. Remove the muslin.

III. Record the Pattern Shape

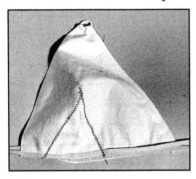
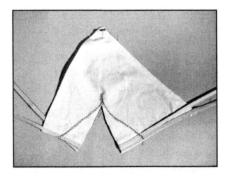
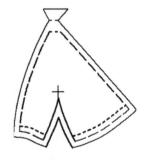

1. Zigzag the edges of the dart, as indicated by the black stitching in the photo.
2. Cut through the center of the dart shape and spread the muslin flat.
3. Transfer the dart shape from the muslin to a paper pattern.
4. Make a second pattern for the foam with no seam allowances, as indicated by the blue lines.

Sewing Darts and Seams

For bras and bikinis there is a standard way of sewing seams and darts over the breast to keep them flat.

Sewing Darts
1. Sew the dart with a straight stitch or, if there is some stretch in the fabric, a 1 mm zigzag.
2. Press the dart to the side of the body, then use a 2 mm zigzag to topstitch the dart allowance flat.
3. Trim off the excess dart allowance.

Sewing Seams
1. Sew the seam with a straight stitch or, if there is some stretch in the fabric, a 1 mm zigzag.
2. Press the open, then use a 2 mm zigzag to topstitch the seam allowances flat.
3. Trim off the excess seam allowance.

Bikini Top Designs

Once you have created the basic pattern, it may be used to create a variety of garments. The three basic design variations described in this chapter are:
- Gathered Bikini Tops
- Darted Bikini Tops
- Princess Seam Bikini Tops

Additional looks can be achieved using different finishing details for swimsuits and daywear.
- Bikini Bras
- Single Cord Bikini Tops
- Double Cord Bikini Tops
- Elasticized Bikini Tops
- Fashion Fabric Tied Bikini Tops
- Ring Bikini Tops

By adding a skirt below the rib cage you can create short tops, lingerie, dresses, and full length gowns.

Gathered Swimsuit Top

Darted Swimsuit Top

Bikini Bra

Ring Swimsuit Top

Lingerie

Day Dress

Sewing Basics

There are a few basic sewing techniques used to create the finished garments in this book. Elastic is frequently used to finish the edges of a garment. This elastic might also provide some shaping to the edges of a garment to enhance the three-dimensional aspect of the fit. Cording is used for some garments. It may be purchased in colors or made from the fashion fabric of the garment.

Non-Decorative Elastic

Non-decorative elastic is used in different widths: 1/4" (6 mm), 1/2" (12 mm), or 3/4" (18 mm).

1. Pin the elastic on the wrong side of the fabric close to the edge.
2. If the elastic is narrow, zigzag down the middle of the elastic. If the elastic is wide, zigzag the edge of the elastic that is opposite the edge.
3. Turn the elastic to the inside of the fabric and zigzag in place. If the elastic is wide, zigzag the edge opposite the turned side.

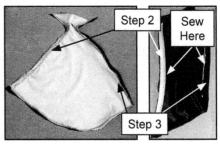

Sewing Elastic

Decorative Elastic

Decorative elastic has one plain edge and one picot edge. The side of the elastic that will be next to the skin is usually plush. The elastic allowance added to the pattern for the garment should be adjusted to the width of the elastic.

1. Pin the elastic on the right side of the fabric close to the edge. The picot edge of the elastic should be facing away from the edge of the fabric. The plush side should be face up.
2. Use a 2 mm zigzag stitch to sew the elastic to the fabric. The stitching should be just inside the edge of the decorative picot.
3. Trim off the excess elastic allowance.
4. Turn the elastic to the inside of the fabric and zigzag in place. As this stitching will be seen on the face of the garment, select a zigzag stitch, such as a three step zigzag, that you want for the design.

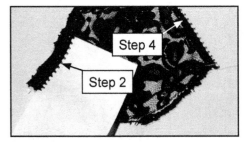

Decorative, Neckline Elastic

Fashion Fabric Cording

Fashion fabric cording can be made from either woven or knit fabric. Woven should be cut on the bias and knit should be cut with the width in the direction of maximum stretch. The cord will need to be at least twice as long as the length of the fashion fabric.

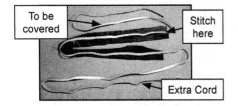

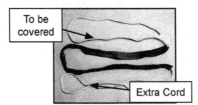

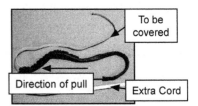

1. Cut the fashion fabric the desired length and wide enough to go around the cord plus 1" (25 mm) for seam allowance.
2. Mark the length of the cording on the cord.
3. Stitch one end of the fabric to the cord at this mark, wrong side out.

4. Use a zipper foot and a 1 mm zigzag to sew the fashion fabric around the cord.
5. Trim off the excess seam allowance.

6. Pull the fashion fabric right side out. Depending on the amount of stretch in the fashion fabric this can be a time consuming process.

Gathered Bikini Top

The Gathered Bikini Top can be made by following the same instructions for making a trial muslin Bikini Top, see page 14. This example uses doubled cording around the neck. The fashion fabric is lined.

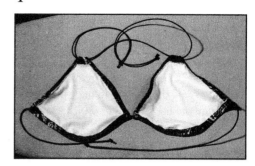

Sewing Instructions

1. Cut 2 Bikini Tops out of the fashion fabric. If you are using stretch fabric, the direction of greatest stretch should be around the body.
2. If you are using a lining, cut two Bikini Tops out of the lining, then use a 4 mm zigzag to attach the lining to the fashion fabric around the edges.
3. Cut 1/4" (6 mm) elastic for the two sides of each Bikini top. The elastic should be slightly shorter than the distance from the top to the bottom of the Bikini Top.
4. Pin the elastic on the wrong side of the fabric, then zigzag the elastic.
5. Turn the elastic to the inside of the Bikini and zigzag in place.
6. Fold over the top of the Bikini Top. If you are using a ring, thread it through the top.
7. Use a zipper foot and a straight stitch to topstitch the top of the Bikini Top for the cording or the ring.
8. Change back to a regular presser foot and zigzag just below the topstitching from Step 7.
9. Cut cording that is the circumference of the rib cage plus 24" (60 cm) for ties.
10. Sew a 1 mm zigzag stitch to indicate the finished bottom edge of the Bikini Top.
11. Turn the bottom seam allowance for the cord casing to the inside of the Bikini with the cord inside, then hand baste the casing in place.
12. Sew a stretch stitch or 1 mm zigzag to encase the cording. Using a zipper foot will help hold the cord in place while you sew.
13. Sew a 3 mm zigzag just above the stitching from Step 12.
14. Trim the seam allowances close to the zigzag stitching.
15. For a double cord Bikini Top, measure the distance from the top of one bikini to the top of the other side, then double the measurement. Add 24" (60 cm) to this length for ties, then cut a cord this length.
16. For a Bikini Top with rings, measure from the top of the bikini to the neck at Center Back then add 12" (30 cm) for ties, then cut two lengths.
17. Either thread the neck cord through the top of the Bikini or tie it to the rings.

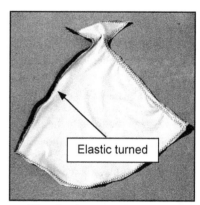

Elastic zigzagged to sides

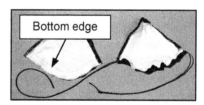

Cording channel

Corded Bikini Top

This corded Bikini Top uses cording made from fashion fabric. The length of the cording for the rib cage should be the distance around the rib cage plus 24" (60 cm) for ties. The cording for the neck should be twice the distance around the neck from Bikini Top to Bikini Top plus 24" (60 cm) for ties. If you are going to sew the cording to the Bikini Top and use only a single length of cord around the neck, add 12" (30 cm) to the length from the top of the bikini to the Center Back of the neck.

The instructions below show how to create the Bikini Top with foam. The use of foam and/or lining material is optional. Depending on the nature of the fashion fabric and the body of the person who will wear the bikini, you may want to try fitting the Bikini Top with and without foam to determine the most suitable shaping and control.

Sewing Instructions

1. Create the fashion fabric cording, see page 18 for details.
2. Use the pattern that does not include seam allowance to cut two pieces of foam.
3. Use the pattern with seam allowances to cut two pieces of fashion fabric and two pieces of lining.
4. Zigzag the foam to the lining around all the edges of the foam.
5. Pin the dart in the lining, then sew. Sew just outside the edge of the foam. This way the edges of the foam will butt together without adding any additional bulk.
6. Press the wedge of the dart to the inside of the Bikini Top, then topstitch with either a straight stitch or a zigzag.
7. Trim off the excess wedge of the dart.
8. Pin the dart in the fashion fabric, then sew.
9. Press the wedge of the dart to the outside of the Bikini Top, then topstitch with either a straight stitch or a zigzag. If you do not want exposed topstitching, this step is optional.
10. Trim off the excess wedge of the dart.
11. Baste the fashion fabric to the lining, wrong sides together. The foam becomes sandwiched between the lining and the fashion fabric.
12. Sew around the outside edges using a 4 mm zigzag stitch.
13. Sew the elastic to the wrong sides of the Bikini Top, stretching the elastic slightly while you sew.
14. Turn the elastic to the inside of the Bikini Top and topstitch in place with a 3 mm zigzag stitch.
15. Turn the top of the bikini over the neck cording then zigzag in place.
16. Trim off any excess seam allowance at the top of the bikini.
17. Sew the cording channel using a straight stitch close to the cording.
18. Sew a second line of 4 mm zigzag stitching just up from the cording.
19. Baste the rib cage cording to the bottom of the bikini.
20. Using a straight stitch close to the cording, sew the cording channel.
21. Sew a second line of 4 mm zigzag stitching just up from the cording.

Foam zigzagged to lining

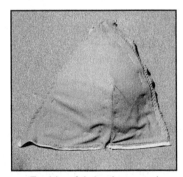

Fashion fabric zigzagged to lining

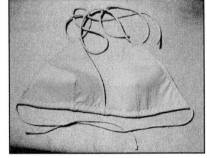

Finished Bikini Top

Tied Bikini Tops

The Tied Bikini Top has fashion fabric for the ties.

For the tie around the neck, measure from the Bikini Top up to the Center Back of the neck and add 12" (30 cm) for the tie. Cut these ties twice the finished width plus 1" (25 mm) for two 1/2" (12 mm) seam allowances.

For the tie around the rib cage, add 24" (60 cm) to the rib cage measurement. Cut these ties twice the finished width plus 1" (25 mm) for two 1/2" (12 mm) seam allowances.

 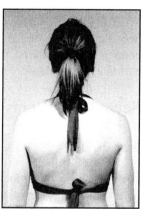

Sewing Instructions

1. Cut two tops out of the fashion fabric. If you are using stretch fabric, the direction of greatest stretch should be around the body.
2. If you are using a lining, cut two tops out of the lining, then zigzag the lining to the fashion fabric.
3. Pin the dart, then sew.
4. From the inside, press the wedge of the dart to the outside of the bikini, then topstitch with either a straight stitch or a zigzag.
5. Trim off the excess wedge of the dart.
6. Fold one of the neck ties in half, right sides together, and pin, then sew.
7. Trim the seam allowance of the tie, then turn the tie right side out.
8. Pin the end of the tie to the top of the bikini, right sides together, then sew.
9. Using a 3 mm zigzag stitch, sew elastic to the side seam allowances of the top.
10. Turn the elastic to the inside of the bikini, then topstitch along the sides using a 4 mm zigzag.
11. Pin the tops to the center of the rib cage tie, right sides together, then sew.
12. Pin a length of twill tape to the bottom seam allowance of the bikini, then sew.
13. Fold one end of the rib cage tie in half, right sides together, then pin.
14. Sew from one end of the tie to the body of the bikini.
15. Trim the seam allowance of the tie, then turn the tie right side out.
16. Repeat steps 13 through 15 with the other side.
17. Enclose the top of the bikini inside the tie, then hand baste in place.
18. Topstitch the tie along the bottom of the bikinis with a 2 mm zigzag stitch.

Sewing Darts

Sewing Neck Tie

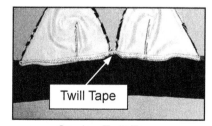

Twill Tape

Sewing Twill Tape

The Bikini Bra

The Bikini Top pattern can be used to create a bra. The main difference between the Bikini Top as a swimsuit and as a bra is the use of bra making notions: bra strap elastic, bra sliders and rings, a bra clasp or G-hook, and neckline edging elastic.

Sewing Bra Straps to Sliders, Rings, or Clasps

When you are sewing Bra Straps to Bra Sliders, Rings, or Clasps, follow these steps:
1. Pull 1" (25 mm) of the strap through the clasp, slider, or ring.
2. Use a zipper foot to sew 2 mm straight stitches close to the edge of the clasp, slider, or ring.
3. Switch to a regular foot, then sew a 2 mm long, 4 mm zigzag stitch to prevent the strap from raveling.

Qty	Materials
1	12" (30 cm) Square of Fabric
3	3/4" (20 mm) Bra Rings
4	3/4" (20 mm) Bra Sliders
2 yds	3/4" Bra Strap Elastic

I. The Pattern
1. Add 1/4" (6 mm) seam allowances to the two sides of the basic Bikini Top pattern.
2. Add a 1" (25 mm) wide by 1" (25 mm) long overlap allowance to the top of the Bikini Top pattern for a ring.
3. Add a 1/2" (12 mm) elastic allowance to the bottom of the Bikini Top pattern.
4. Cut the Bikini Top pattern out of the fashion fabric (and optional lace).

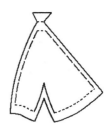

II. Prepare the Fashion Fabric & Sew the Dart

The Bikini Bra may be made from a single layer of fashion fabric or it may be a combination of lace and a fashion fabric. Tricot is used in this example. For the purposes of these instructions, once lace is added to the solid fabric, the combined fabric will be referred to as the fashion fabric.
1. If you are using two layers, such as lace over a solid color, pin the lace to the fashion fabric, then sew a 4 mm zigzag around the edges.
2. If you are using multiple layers for the top, sew a line of stay stitching along the center line of the dart.
3. Pin the dart, then sew.
4. From the inside, press the wedge of the dart to the outside of the Bikini Top, then topstitch with either a straight stitch or a zigzag.
5. Trim off the excess wedge of the dart.
6. If you are using lining with foam, combine it to the fashion fabric. If you are not using a lining, skip this step.
7. Pin the fashion fabric to the lining.
8. Sew around the outside edges using a 4 mm zigzag stitch.

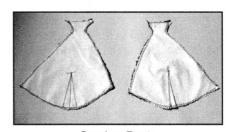

Sewing Darts

IV. Neckline Elastic

The Bikini Bra shown uses a fancy picot neckline elastic on the sides of the Bikini Top. There are two sides to this elastic: the decorative side with the Picot edge; and the main body of the elastic which is solid. The idea is to attach the elastic so that the main body of the elastic is turned to the inside of the Bikini Top, leaving the decorative edge exposed. The finished edge of fashion fabric should appear at the center of the elastic.

1. Pin the elastic to the inside edge of the Bikini Top. The decorative edge should be facing into the middle of the Bikini Top. If you are not using foam, align the outside of the elastic to the outside of the Bikini Top. If you are using foam, align the center of the elastic to the edge of the foam.
2. Sew the elastic to the fashion fabric with a 2 mm zigzag down the center of the elastic. These zigzag stitches should not lap over onto the decorative edge of the elastic.
3. From the inside, trim off the excess seam allowance.
4. Turn the elastic to the inside of the Bikini Top and hand baste in place so the decorative edge is positioned correctly.
5. From the good side of the Bikini Top, topstitch the edge of the Bikini Top with a 4 mm zigzag stitch.
6. Repeat Steps 11 through 15 for the outside elastic.

Neckline Elastic

V. Bikini Top Ring

This design uses a ring at the top of the Bikini for the neck strap.

1. Thread the top of the bikini through a ring. A 3/4" (20 mm) ring is used in this example.
2. Use a zipper foot to sew a line of straight stitches close to the edge of the ring.
3. Switch to a regular foot and sew a line of 4 mm zigzag stitches close to the edge of the ring.
4. From the inside, trim off any excess overlap fabric.

Bra Strap Ring

VI. Bottom Edge of the Bikini Top

The bottom edge of the Bikini Top is finished with 1/2" (12 mm) bra strap elastic on the outside and 1/2" (12 mm) twill tape on the inside. This design uses a Bra Front Clasp at Center Front and a 1/2" (12 mm) ring on the outside edge of the Bikini Top.

1. Loop one end of a length of Bra Strap through one side of the clasp, then sew as described on page 22.
2. Pin a length of twill tape to the bottom edge of the Bikini Top. This will position it over the elastic allowance.
3. Use a 2 mm zigzag stitch to sew the top edge of the twill tape to the Bra Top.
4. Trim off the excess seam allowance.
5. Hold the clasp close to the Center Front edge of a Bikini Top and determine the length necessary for the strap to reach the Bikini Top's side. Allow for a 1" (25 mm) overlap to sew a ring.
6. Cut two straps to the length determined in step 5.
7. On the ends of these straps opposite the Bra Clasp, sew 1/2" (12 mm) Rings using the 1" (25 mm) overlap.

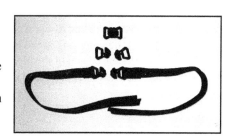

Bra Front Clasp

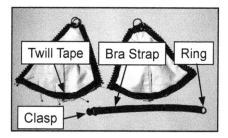

Twill Tape   Bra Strap   Ring

Clasp

Rib Cage Bra Strap

VI. Bottom Edge of the Bikini Top, cont'd

8. Starting at the front edge, hand baste the elastic to the good side of the Bikini Top.
9. Use a 2 mm zigzag to topstitch the top edge of the elastic to the Bikini Top.
10. Use a 4 mm zigzag stitch to topstitch the bottom edge of the elastic to the twill tape.

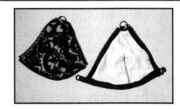

Sewn Bra Strap

VII. Add the Straps

To allow the tension of the rib cage elastic to be adjusted in the back, use a bra strap ring and two bra strap sliders. Add 1/2" (12 mm) bra straps at the rib cage and the neck.

1. Measure the distance from one side of the Bikini Top to the other, then subtract this from the Rib Cage elastic measurement.
2. Divide this measurement in half, then add 4" for adjustments and overlap.
3. Use the measurement from step 2 to cut two lengths of Bra Strap. These will be the Rib Cage Straps.
4. Loop one end of the Rib Cage strap around the middle bar of a Bra Strap Slider, then sew as described on page 22.
5. Thread the free end of the Rib Cage Straps through a ring, then secure the strap through the slider.
6. Repeat steps 4 and 5 for the other Rib Cage Elastic.
7. To attach the Rib Cage Strap to the Bikini Top, thread the free end of the Rib Cage Strap through the ring, then sew as described on page 22.
8. Double the measurement from the spinal column of the wearer to the top of the Bikini Top and add 4" for adjustments and overlap.
9. Cut a length of Bra Strap as determined in Step 8. This will be the Neck Strap.
10. Loop one end of the Neck Strap around the middle bar of a Bra Strap Slider, then sew as described on page 22.
11. Thread the free end of the Neck Strap through a ring at the top of one side of the Bikini Bra, then secure the strap through the slider.
12. Thread the free end of the Neck Strap through another slider, then through the other ring at the top of the Bikini Bra.
13. Thread the free end of the Neck Strap through the middle bar of the slider, then sew as described on page 22.

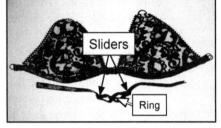

Rib Cage Strap

Sewn Rib Cage Strap

Neck Strap

Finished Bikini Bra

Draping a Princess Seam Bikini Top

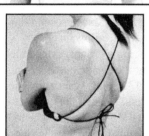

Depending on the wearer's body and the material used, a dart in a Bikini Top may not fit all the contours. The photo to the right shows how a muslin Bikini Top with a dart leaves a gap on the side. This gap can be eliminated with stretch fabric, tension when the elastic is sewn, or with a princess seam.

The instructions below show how to create a Princess Seam Bikini Top that conforms closely to the contours of the body. This example uses velvet Lycra with rings at the top, center, and sides of the bikini. Cording is tied to the rings. The cording can either be separated into neck and rib cage ties, Or, the cording can cross the back and return from the sides to be tied once at the Center Back.

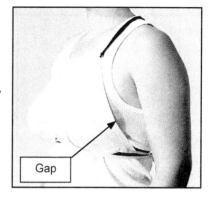

Gap

I. Draping the Pattern Shape

To drape a Bikini Top with a Princess Seam, use bias tapes and Velcro. Cut a square of muslin, then follow the steps below.

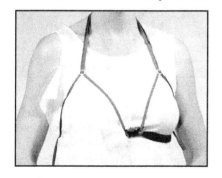

1. Place the muslin under the bias tapes.

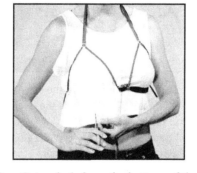

2. Cut a slash from the bottom of the muslin to the Bust Apex.

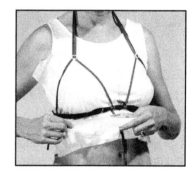

3. Close the dart with masking tape.

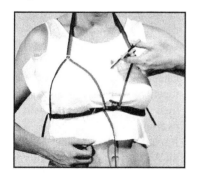

4. Cut the muslin from the inside of the Bikini Top almost to the Bust Apex, then tape it closed.

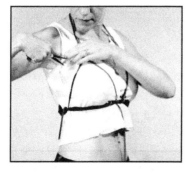

5. Cut the muslin from the outside of the Bikini Top almost to the Bust Apex, then tape it closed.

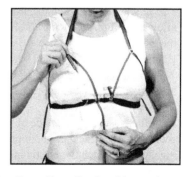

6. Draw lines for the sides and bottom of the Bikini Top.

25

II. Create the Pattern

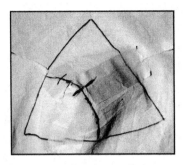
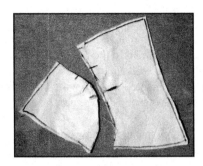
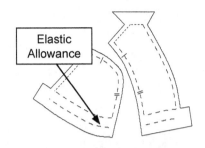

Elastic Allowance

1. On the muslin, draw a line, as illustrated, from the side of the bikini, through the Apex, and down to the rib cage. This is the princess seam line.
2. Draw sewing notches across the princess seam line.

3. Cut the muslin along the lines drawn for the bikini shape and the princess seam line, then flatten the two muslin pieces.
4. Trace the muslin shapes onto a piece of pattern paper.

5. Add the width of the 3/4" (20 mm) rib cage elastic to the bottom of the patterns, then draw a second line for the elastic allowance.
6. For the ring overlaps, extend the lines for the elastic out 1" (25 mm).
7. Add 1/4" (6 mm) seam allowances to the remainder of the pattern.
8. Add a 1" (25 mm) flap to the top of the pattern for securing the ring.

III. Sew the Bikini Top

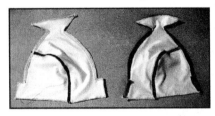
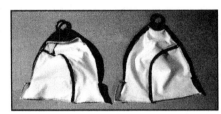

1. Use the patterns to cut the fashion fabric and the lining material.
2. Sew the lining fabric to the fashion fabric using a 4 mm zigzag stitch.
3. Pin the fabric along the princess seam, right sides together, then sew with a 1 mm zigzag stitch.
4. Press open and use a 2 mm zigzag stitch to topstitch the seam allowance in place, then trim off the excess seam allowance.
5. Using a 3 mm zigzag stitch, sew 1/4" (6 mm) elastic along the inside and outside edges of the Swimsuit Top's wrong side.
6. Turn the elastic to the inside of the Swimsuit Top, then sew a 3 mm zigzag to topstitch the elastic in place.

7. Thread a ring through the top of the Swimsuit Top, then pin the overlap in place.
8. Use a zipper foot to sew the ring in place with a straight stitch.
9. Change to a regular foot and topstitch with a 2 mm zigzag stitch, then trim off the excess overlap.

10. On the wrong side of the fabric, sew the 3/4" (20 mm) elastic to the bottom of the Swimsuit Top along the lower edge.
11. Turn the elastic to the inside, then topstitch it along the top edge of the elastic.
12. Thread a ring through the elastic on the outside of the Swimsuit Top, then pin the overlap in place.
13. Use a zipper foot to sew the ring in place with a straight stitch.
14. Change to a regular foot and topstitch with a 2 mm zigzag stitch, then trim off the excess elastic overlap.
15. Repeat Steps 12 through 14 to sew all the rings to the Swimsuit Top.

Finished Bikini Top

Adding a Skirt to the Bikini Top

The Bikini Top pattern can be used to create tops, dresses, and gowns. To create the body for these gowns, use rectangles of muslin that have vertical lines of stay stitching for the Center Front and Center Back lines, then drape muslin from the rib cage down to the hem.

Drape the Bikini Top Skirt

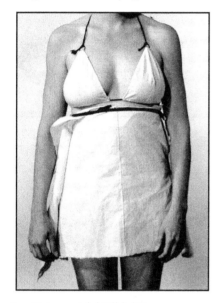
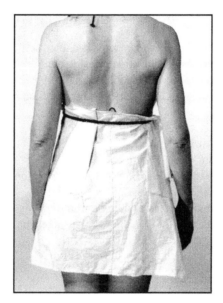

1. Put on a trial Bikini Top.
2. Place a length of Velcro around the waist to hold up the muslin.
3. Tuck a square of muslin for the front under the Velcro.
4. Verify the Center Front is hanging straight down the body.

5. Tuck a second square of muslin under the Velcro in the back.
6. Verify the Center Back is hanging straight down the body.
7. Smooth the fabric to the side. For a fitted garment, you may add a hip dart, then pin the location for point of the dart.

8. Establish the side seam by folding back the front muslin along the desired seam line, then pin in place.
9. To indicate the rib cage seam, draw a line from Center Front to Center Back.
10. Remove the muslin and trace the shapes to make a paper pattern.

Bikini Top Dress

For the skirt of a Bikini Dress, use the pattern created from the instructions on page 27. Adjust the hem to the desired length. This hem can be established when the skirt is first assembled or as a final step.

For this example, the skirt has a Center Front seam to take advantage of the vertical pattern on the fabric. For the Bikini Top and the rib cage band, fashion fabric is also used as the lining fabric. The rib cage band should be the rib cage measurement, plus 1" (25 mm) of ease, plus a 1-1/2" (40 mm) hook and eye overlap, plus two seam allowances. The width of the rib cage band is a design decision.

Sewing Instructions for the Bikini Top Dress

This example is made from woven fabric. All the sewing is done with straight stitches except as noted.

1. Fold one of the neck ties in half, right sides together, and pin, then sew.
2. Trim the seam allowance of the tie, then turn the tie right side out.
3. Pin the dart in the fashion fabric, then sew as described on page 16.
4. On one of the Bikini Tops, pin the strap to the right side of the fashion fabric.
5. Pin a lining piece to the fashion fabric, right sides together, then sew along the sides and top of the Bikini Top. The strap is sandwiched between the two layers of the Bikini Top.
6. Use a zigzag stitch to sew elastic to the two sides of the Bikini Top along the seam allowances.
7. Pin the Bikini Tops between the fashion fabric and lining of the rib cage band, right sides together. Sew along the full length of the rib cage band.
8. Add a zipper to the Center Back seam of the Bikini Dress skirt.
9. Pin the front and back skirt panels along the side seams, right sides together, then sew.
10. Pin the skirt to the fashion fabric of the rib cage band, right sides together, then sew.
11. Turn the rib cage lining down to enclose the top of the skirt seam allowance, then sew in place using a hand sewn blind hem stitch.
12. Sew a hook and eye to the Center Back overlap.
13. Hem the skirt.

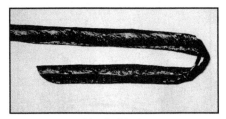

Neck Strap

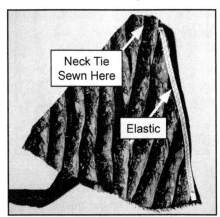

Neck Tie Sewn Here

Elastic

Sewing Bikini Top

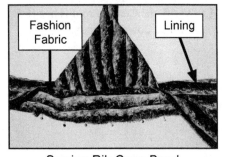

Fashion Fabric

Lining

Sewing Rib Cage Band

Baby Doll Nightgown

A Baby Doll Nightgown can be made by combining the Bikini Top with a "skirt."

The design shown here uses elastic cording the same color as the fabric. There are two cords. One cord goes down the inside of the Bikini Top. The other cord goes down the outside of the Bikini Top and around the back. Both cords tie at the back of the neck.

Matching lace may be topstitched to both the Bikini Top and the hem as illustrated.

I. The Pattern

These instructions show how to add enough allowance to the Bikini Top pattern to create a channel for elastic cording. For the "skirt," use the pattern created from the instructions on page 27. You can extend this "skirt" to any length–from a short top to a full length gown.

While the design shown here is for a short top cut from chiffon, there is no reason the "skirt" pattern can't be lengthened or made from flannel so long as you make sure you have adequate ease around the hips. If you are using a woven fabric, you must add enough fullness to the back pattern at the rib cage so the top can be pulled over the hips. For instructions on how to add fullness to the hem, see page 50.

1. On a copy of the Bikini Top pattern, add 1" (25 mm) cording allowance to the two sides. Add a 1/2" (12 mm) seam allowance to the bottom edge.
2. On a copy of the skirt pattern, extend the pattern to the length desired.
3. If you are using woven fabric, increase the width of the back pattern so the combined rib cage of the front and back skirt is slightly larger than the wearer's hip measurement.
4. Add 1/2" (12 mm) seam allowances to the skirt pattern's edges.

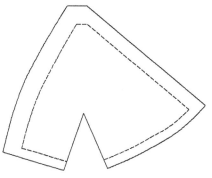

Bikini Top Pattern

II. Sewing Basics

For the Baby Doll style in chiffon, I recommend cutting the fabric for the skirt on the fold or else the seam will be clearly visible. For the Baby Doll chiffon skirt's side seams, use a French Seam.

1. Pin the pattern for the Bikini Top to the fashion fabric, then cut two.
2. Pin the front pattern for the skirt to the fashion fabric, then cut one.
3. Pin the back pattern for the skirt to the fashion fabric, then cut one.
4. Pin the front skirt to the back skirt and sew the side seams.
5. The hem of the skirt can be sewn at this point or later. This example uses a rolled hem.
6. Sew the darts in the Bikini Tops.
7. If you are sewing chiffon, press the wedge of the dart material to the outside, then topstitch with a 2 mm zigzag next to the dart stitching.
8. From the inside, trim the dart wedge close to the zigzagged topstitching.

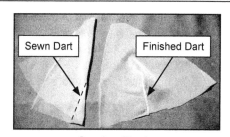

Sewn Dart | Finished Dart

Sewing Darts

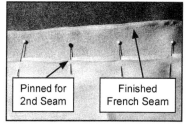

Pinned for 2nd Seam | Finished French Seam

French Side Seam

III. Sew the Inside Edge of the Baby Doll Top

The inside neckline of this Baby Doll Top uses an elastic cord inside channeling. This cording should be long enough to go from the back of the neck to the rib cage and back to the neck. As you will need two ties, add 24" (60 cm) to the overall length of this cording.

The instructions below are for adding the cording to the front neckline before sewing the tops to the skirt. An alternate approach would be to sew the tops to the skirt, then add the cording.

1. Press the Bikini Top's top seam allowance to the inside.
2. Press the inside channel allowance of the Bikini Top to the inside.
3. Cut the cording for the front neckline. This should be twice the distance from the rib cage to the spinal column plus 12" (30 cm) for ties.
4. To establish the center, tie an overhand knot in the middle of the cording.
5. Place the cording inside the channel allowance for one side of the front neckline.
6. With a zipper foot, sew the channeling close to the cord with a straight stitch. Do not catch the cord with your stitching.
7. With a blind hem foot, sew the channel allowance with a 2 mm zigzag stitch.
8. From the inside, trim the excess channel allowance down to the zigzag stitching from Step 7.
9. To sew the channeling for the other Bikini Top, follow Steps 5 to 8. Verify you have a left and right Bikini Top.

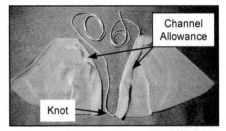

Sewing Cording to the Inside Edge

IV. Sew the Bikini Top to the Skirt

Before you sew the top to the skirt, sew a reinforcing tab at Center Front. This will prevent the Center Front from ripping in case any strain is placed on the garment's rib cage. It can be made from a 1" (25 mm) square of fabric.

1. Pin a tab of fabric to the Center Front of the skirt, right sides together.
2. Sew a square "U" in the fabric that is 1/2" (12 mm) tall and 1/4" (6 mm) wide at the bottom.
3. Clip through the center of the "U" to about 1/8" from the bottom of the "U".
4. Clip from the center of the "U" to the corners.
5. Turn the tab to the inside and press.
6. Pin the Bikini Top to the skirt, right sides together, starting from Center Front.
7. Following Steps 2 to 6, sew a second reinforcing tab on the skirt at the Bikini Top's side.
8. Sew the Bikini Top to the skirt.
9. Press the seam allowance down on top of the skirt.
10. From the good side, topstitch the seam allowance using a 2 mm zigzag stitch.
11. From the inside, trim the seam allowance to the zigzag stitching.
12. Repeat Steps 6 through 11 for the other Bikini Top.

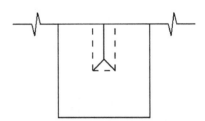

Reinforcing Tab Pattern

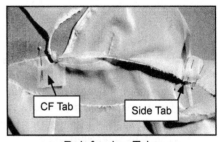

Reinforcing Tabs

Side Tab Close Up

V. Finishing the Baby Doll

Use elastic cording for the outside and back of the Baby Doll top so the garment can be pulled over the head. Measure from the spinal column at the neck around the side of the Bikini Top and down the Center Back to the rib cage line. Double this length, and then, for ties, add 24" (60 cm). Cut the elastic cording to this length.

1. Place the cording inside the channeling for the side of the Bikini Top, then hand baste in place.
2. Continue around the back of the skirt, hand basting the channel allowance in place.
3. Continue up the side of the other Bikini Top, hand basting the channeling in place.
4. Use a zipper foot to sew the channeling in place.
5. Use a blind hem foot to zigzag the channeling allowance in place.
6. From the inside, trim the channeling allowance of the Bikini Tops to the zigzagging.
7. To add rows of fringe to the Baby Doll Top, pin and then sew with a 3 mm zigzag stitch.

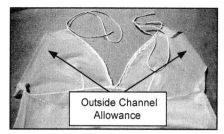

Outside Channels

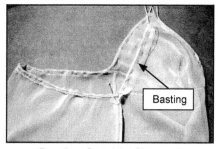

Basting Outside Channel

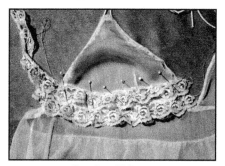

Sewing Fringe

Finished Baby Doll

Bikini Briefs & Thongs

A Bikini Briefs covers the lower torso in front and back without a Side Seam. It can be either a one or two-piece pattern. A Thong can be created from the pattern shape for a Bikini Briefs's front.

For the Bikini Briefs, use bias tape and Velcro to indicate the desired design lines on the body of the person who is to wear the bikini. To create the pattern, you can then measure from key reference points to the design lines. Often, no additional fitting is required.

The Bikini Briefs pattern can be used for diverse designs including:
- Single Cord Bikini Briefs
- Double Cord Bikini Briefs
- Elasticized Bikini Briefs
- Fashion Fabric Tied Bikini Briefs
- Ring Bikini Briefs
- Thong

The Thong described in these instructions uses bra making supplies so it can be adjusted. The look is designed to match the Bikini Bra on page 22.

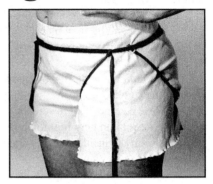

Creating the Design Lines

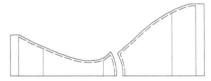

Bikini Bottom Pattern

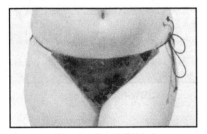

Single Cord Bikini

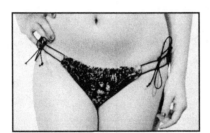

Double Cord Bikini

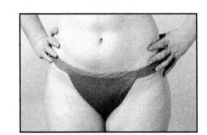

Elasticized Bikini

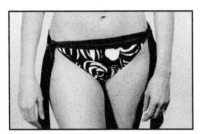

Fashion Tied Bikini

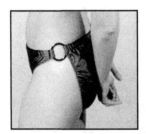

Ring Bikini

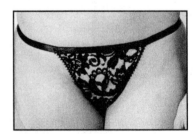

Thong

Creating the Basic Bikini Briefs Pattern

To create a Bikini Briefs pattern, follow the steps below:
1. Create design lines using Velcro and bias tape.
2. Measure where the design lines are located on the body.
3. Use the measurements to draw the pattern.
4. Cut the pattern out of scrap fabric and sew a trial Bikini Briefs.

I. Create the Shape for the Bikini Briefs

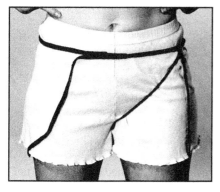 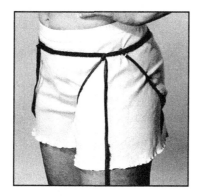 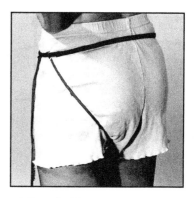

1. Secure Velcro around the waist level desired.

2. Secure one end of the bias tape to the side of the Velcro.
3. Run the bias tape under the leg and tie it in front.

4. Adjust the bias tapes as needed to create the shape of the Bikini Briefs desired.

Bikini Briefs Design Considerations

When you are preparing the design lines for a Bikini Briefs, keep in mind that in a design which follows the crease between buttocks and thigh, the back tends to shift toward the middle of the buttocks as you move.

To avoid this, position the design lines as illustrated.

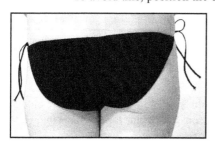 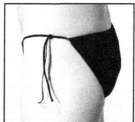 

Briefs has moved up buttocks

Design follows the crease between buttocks and thigh.

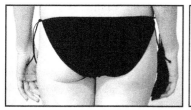 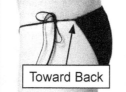 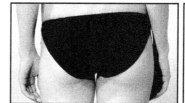 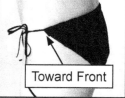

Toward Back

Toward Front

Design follows the middle of the buttocks.

Design carries the back forward.

II. Measure and Draft the Bikini Briefs

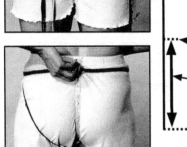

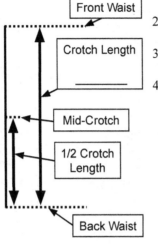

Front Waist

Crotch Length
_____

Mid-Crotch

1/2 Crotch Length

Back Waist

1. Measure the length of the crotch from the Velcro at Center Front to the Velcro at Center Back.
2. Draw a vertical line that is the Crotch Length. This will be the Center line.
3. Draw horizontal lines at the top and bottom of the center line for the Front and Back Waist lines
4. Draw another horizontal line half way between the Front and Back Waist lines. This is the Mid-Crotch line.

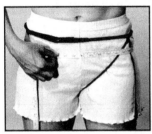

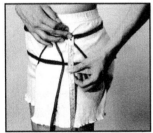

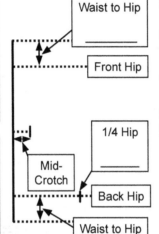

Waist to Hip
_____

Front Hip

1/4 Hip
_____

Mid-Crotch

Back Hip

Waist to Hip

5. For the Hip measurement, measure around the fullest part of the hips.
6. Measure the distance from the Hip Measurement to the Velcro around the waist. This is the Waist to Hip measurement.
7. Use the Waist to Hip measurement to draw horizontal lines for the hip.
8. Mark 1/4 of the Hip measurement on the back Hip line.
9. Use the chart below to mark the length of the Mid-Crotch line.

Hips	Mid-Crotch
Up to 37" (96 cm)	2" (5 cm)
38" to 41" (96 to 104 cm)	2-1/4" (5.7 cm)
Over 41" (104 cm)	2-1/2" (6.4 cm)

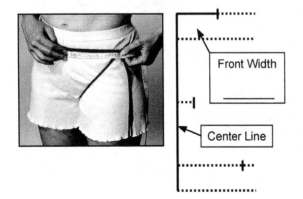

Front Width
_____

Center Line

10. To indicating the side of the Bikini, measure along the Velcro from Center Front to the bias tape. This is the width of the Bikini Briefs's front.
11. Mark this length on the pattern.
12. Draw a solid line from the Center line of the Bikini to this mark. This is the Front Waist line.

II. Measure and Draft the Bikini Briefs, cont'd

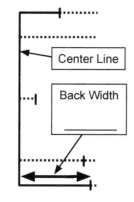

13. To determine the side of the Bikini, measure along the Velcro from Center Back to the bias tape. This is the width of the Bikini Briefs's back.
14. Mark this length on the pattern.
15. Draw a solid line from the Center line of the Bikini to this mark. This is the Back Waist line.

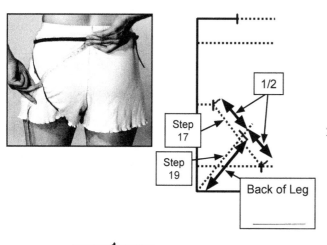

16. Measure diagonally from the Velcro at Center Back to the bias tape around the leg. This is the Back Leg length.
17. Draw a diagonal line from the Mid-Crotch line to the end of the Back Hip line.
18. Divide this diagonal line in half and make a mark.
19. Draw a second diagonal line from the Back Waist line's center through the mark made in Step 18.
20. Mark the Back Leg length on this second diagonal line.

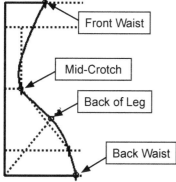

21. Draw the Bikini Briefs's leg opening by connecting the Front Waist line, Mid-Crotch line, Back of Leg mark, and the Back Waist line. The outside edge of Bikini Briefs may or may not intersect with the mark on the back hip line. Record the circumference of the waist and the length of the

Waist Measurement & Elastic

Waist Measurement _____

Waist Elastic _____

elastic for the waist.

1. Measure the distance around the waist at the Velcro. This is the Waist measurement.
2. For a Bikini Briefs's waist band, place an elastic around the waist line and adjust it for the wearer's comfort level, then record the length.

III. Creating a Two Piece Pattern (optional)

To create a two-piece pattern for a Bikini Briefs, follow the steps below:

1. Align your one-piece pattern with the diagram to the right so that it touches the Center and Mid-Crotch lines.
2. Trace the curved hip seam line onto the one-piece pattern.
3. Lay a fresh sheet of paper on top of the one-piece pattern.
4. Trace the front pattern.
5. Slide the paper for the new pattern up 1" (25 mm) to leave room for seam allowances.
6. Trace the back pattern.

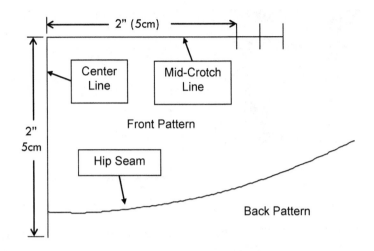

IV. Add Casing and Seam Allowances

Add seam allowances for the elastic at the leg opening and a casing allowance for the waist. Elastic is stretched when added to the back of a leg opening to shape the fabric over the buttocks, so the elastic should be 2" (5 cm) shorter than the length of the pattern's leg opening.

1. Add 1/4" (6 mm) seam allowances to the seams that join the front to the back.
2. Add 1/4" (6 mm) elastic allowances to the leg openings.
3. Add 1/2" (12 mm) casing allowances to the front and back waist lines.
4. For a two-piece pattern, add 1/4" (6 mm) seam allowances to the hip seams.

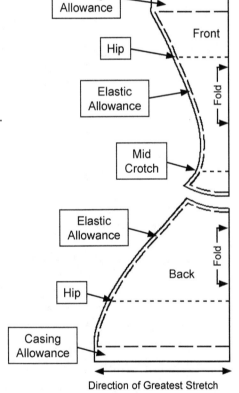

V. Sewing the Bikini Briefs

Bikini Briefs usually don't require any fitting adjustments. However, it is always a good idea to test the pattern in scrap fabric.

To stabilize the sides of the Bikini Briefs, sew 1/4" (6 mm) elastic along the edges. When you are sewing elastic, use 100% polyester thread and ballpoint needles in your sewing machine. These instructions show how to make a trial Bikini Briefs out of muslin. The photo of the finished briefs shows a shoe lace used for cording.

Qty	Materials
2 yds	1/4" (6 mm) Elastic
1	Fabric as required
2 yds	Cording (or shoe laces)

1. Use the pattern to cut fabric for the Bikini Briefs.
2. For a two-piece Bikini Briefs, sew the front of the bikini to the back at the crotch seam.
3. Cut 1/4" (6 mm) elastic for the Bikini leg openings. The elastic should be 2" (5 cm) shorter than the leg opening on the pattern.
4. Pin the elastic on the wrong side of the fabric, then zigzag the elastic to the fashion fabric. Stretch the elastic when sewing the briefs's back.
5. Turn the elastic to the inside of the Bikini and zigzag in place.
6. For the ties, cut cording that is the waist measurement plus 24" (60 cm).
7. Turn the seam allowance for the cord casing to the inside of the Bikini with the cord inside, then hand baste the casing in place.
8. Using a small stitch, zigzag the cord casing. A hem foot will help hold the cord in place while you sew.
9. Trim the cording's seam allowances close to the zigzag stitching.

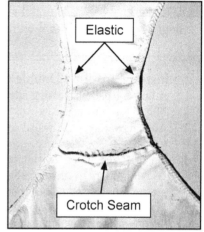

Elastic Zigzagged to Inside

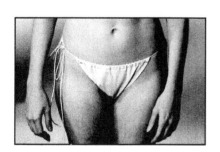

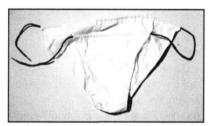

Briefs with Shoe Lace Cord

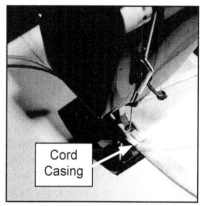

Zigzagging the Cord Casing

Corded Bikini Briefs

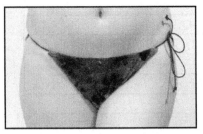

Single Cord Bikini Briefs

A Single Cord Bikini Briefs can be made the same way as the muslin trial Bikini Briefs on page 37.

These instructions are for a two-piece pattern with doubled cording at the sides. To anchor the ties, the fashion fabric is lined with elastic at the waist.

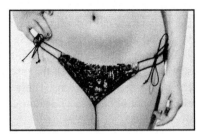

Double Cord Bikini Briefs

Sewing Instructions for a Double Corded Briefs

1. Adjust the pattern's casing allowance to the width of the elastic used. This is the waistband.
2. Add an overlap to the waistband that is the width of the elastic plus 1/4" (6 mm).
3. Add a 1" (25 mm) extension to the waistband.
4. Use the pattern to cut the fashion fabric and the lining. The direction of greatest stretch should be around the body.
5. For the front of the Bikini, use a 4 mm zigzag to sew the lining to the fashion fabric around the edges, wrong sides together.
6. Pin the back's fashion fabric to the front along the crotch seam, right sides together.
7. Pin the lining for the back to the front along the crotch seam, right sides together.
8. Sew the crotch seam with a stretch stitch.
9. Pin the back fashion fabric to the back lining, wrong sides together, then sew the back edges with a 4 mm zigzag stitch.
10. Cut 1/4" (6 mm) elastic for the Bikini leg openings. The elastic should be 2" (5 cm) shorter than the leg opening on the pattern.
11. Pin the elastic to the lining fabric, then zigzag the elastic to both layers of the fabric. Stretch the elastic when sewing the briefs's back half.
12. Turn the elastic to the inside of the Bikini and zigzag in place.
13. Cut elastic for the front and back waist that is the length of the pattern.
14. Use a 4 mm zigzag to sew the elastic to the wrong side of the fabric.
15. Turn the elastic to the inside of the Bikini and zigzag in place.
16. Turn the 1" (25 mm) waist extensions to the inside and sew in place. A darning needle or similar tool can be used to hold the opening for the cording.
17. Cut two lengths of cording, adding 24" (60 cm) for the ties, then thread through the waist loops.

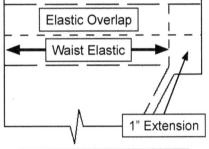

Sewing Crotch Seam

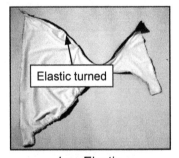

Leg Elastic

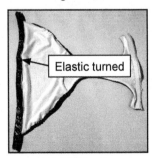

Waist Elastic

Sewing Overlap

38

Elastic & Fashion Tied Bikini Briefs

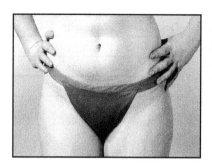

These instructions show how to create Bikini Briefs that use an elastic waist or are tied at the sides. The patterns are divided into front and back sections with lining fabric used for both.

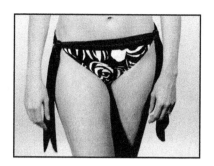

I. Sew the Briefs's Body

1. Pin the back fashion fabric to the back lining, wrong side to wrong side, then use a 4 mm zigzag stitch around all the edges.
2. Pin the front fashion fabric to the back fashion fabric, right sides together, at the crotch seam.
3. Pin the front lining fabric to the wrong side of the back section at the crotch seam, then sew the crotch seam using a stretch stitch or 1 mm zigzag.
4. Pin the front fashion fabric to the front lining, wrong side together, then use a 4 mm zigzag stitch around all the edges.
5. Measure the distance around the leg opening on the pattern. Subtract 2" (50 mm) from this length, then cut two lengths of 1/4" (6 mm) swimsuit elastic.
6. Pin the elastic to the wrong side of the fabric at the leg opening, then sew with a 4 mm zigzag stitch. Stretch the elastic in the area that will be under the buttocks.
7. Turn the elastic to the inside, then topstitch with a 4 mm zigzag.

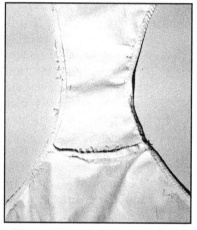

Elastic Sewn to Leg Openings

II. Sew the Waistband

Elastic Waistband

This example includes seams on both sides of the waistband allowing for fine tuning the fit. The waistband becomes a casing for the elastic.

1. Pin the center of the front waistband to the briefs' Center Front, right sides together, then sew.
2. Pin the center of the back waistband to the briefs' Center Back, right sides together, then sew.
3. Sew the Side Seams.
4. Cut the waist elastic using the measurement on page 35, then sew it in a loop.
5. Enclose the elastic in the waistband, then sew the waistband closed.

Tied Waistband

1. Pin the center of the front waistband to the briefs' Center Front, right sides together, then sew.
2. Fold one end of the tie in half, right sides together, then pin.
3. From the end of the tie, sew up to the body of the bikini.
4. Trim the seam allowance of the tie, then turn the tie right side out.
5. Repeat steps 2 through 4 until all the ties are sewn.
6. Enclose the top of the bikini inside the tie, then hand baste in place.
7. Topstitch the tie along the top of the bikini with a 2 mm zigzag stitch.

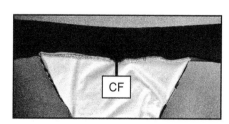

Sew Bikini Front to Tie

Ring Bikini Briefs

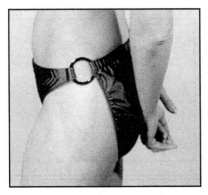

To use a Bikini Briefs pattern to make a Ringed Bikini, the lengths of its front and back patterns need to be adjusted to the position and size of the ring, then an overlap must be added to the pattern for securing the ring.

This example shows how to create the briefs using two pattern pieces. The fashion fabric for the front is lined but not the back.

Qty	Materials
1 yd	1/2" (12 mm) Elastic
1	Fabric as required
2	Swimsuit Rings

Construction of a Ringed Briefs

This example starts with an existing trial muslin Bikini Briefs.

1. Have the wearer put on the trial muslin.
2. Cut two lengths of the waist elastic about 4" (10 cm) longer than half the waist elastic measurement established on page 35.
3. Use the rings to pin the elastic at waist level for the tension desired.
4. To establish the design lines desired, tie a bias tape to one of the rings as shown.
5. Measure the difference between the muslin's location and the new design lines indicated by the bias tape.
6. Use the measurement determined in step 5 to adjust the pattern.
7. Add an overlap to the waistband that is the width of the elastic plus 1/4" (6 mm).
8. Add a 1-1/2" (4 cm) extension to the waistband to secure the rings.

The remainder of the construction process is the same as that for the Double Corded Bikini Briefs described on page 38 starting at step 4.

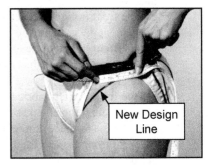

Measure for Ring

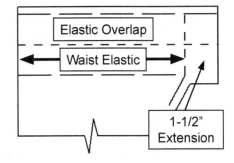

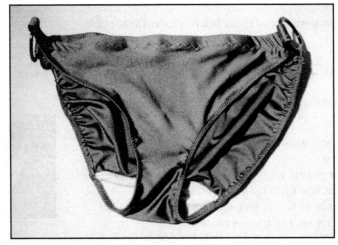

Finished Ring Bikini

Thongs

Thongs can be made in different styles. The pattern described here is created from the Bikini Briefs's front.

The example shown here uses bra strap notions and neckline elastic to create a look that matches the Bikini Bra on page 22.

Qty	Materials
2 yds	1/2" (12 mm) Elastic
1	Fabric as required
3	Bra Strap Sliders
1	Bra Strap Ring

I. The Pattern

1. Put a fresh sheet of pattern paper on top of the Bikini Briefs pattern. Allow enough room on the paper so you can create the full width of the pattern.
2. Draw the waist line for the front.
3. Draw in the mid-crotch position.
4. Taper the front of the bikini to a point.
5. Draw a horizontal line at the bottom of the Thong that is 3/8" (9 mm) wide.
6. Add 1/2" (12 mm) seam allowance to the front and back waistlines.
7. Add 1/4" (6 mm) elastic allowances to both sides.
8. To create a pattern that is the full width of the Thong, fold the paper along the center line and cut.

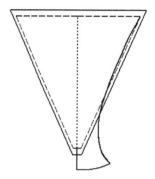

II. Sew the Thong

Thongs can be made from a combination of different fabrics and notions. This example uses a combination of lace and Tricot for the fashion fabric; a woven cotton for the lining.

1. Using the Thong pattern, cut the fashion fabric and lining material.
2. Pin the lace on top of the Tricot, then pin the lining on top of the lace, right sides together.
3. Use a straight stitch to sew the fabric along the top and bottom.
4. Trim off the excess seam allowance.
5. Turn the Thong right side out, then zigzag the sides of the Thong.
6. Sew a slider to a length of bra strap elastic, then thread the bra strap through a ring.
7. Using a 2 mm zigzag stitch, sew neckline elastic along a side of the Thong, right sides together.
8. Trim the excess allowance, then turn the elastic to the inside and topstitch in place.
9. Sew a slider to the waist bra strap elastic, then loop through the ring.
10. Thread a slider through the other end of the bra strap. Thread the strap through the ring. Then sew the bra strap to the center bar of the slider.
11. Center the waist elastic on the front of the thong and topstitch in place.

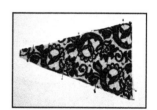

Fabric Combined

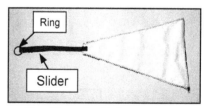

Bra Strap for Between Legs

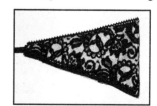

Elastic Edge Finish

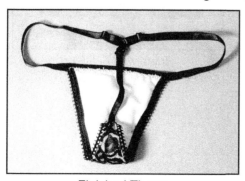

Finished Thong

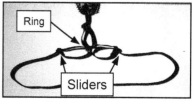

Waistband Elastic

Fitted Briefs

A Fitted Briefs covers the lower torso in front and back and includes Side Seams. It can be worn either as lingerie or swimwear. Basic briefs can have a one, two, or three-piece pattern and can be made in stretch or woven fabric. Variations are created by changing the height of the waist and/or the position of the leg opening, see page 43. These briefs can also be made with a fitted or full skirt.

For the fitted briefs, use bias tape and Velcro to indicate the desired design lines on the body of the person who is to wear the bikini. To create the pattern, you can then measure from key reference points to the design lines. Often, no additional fitting is required..

The Fitted Briefs patterns described in this section include:
- Basic Fitted Briefs (for optional design variations, see page 43)
- Briefs with Fitted Skirt
- Briefs with Full Skirt

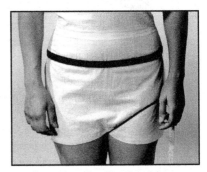
Creating the Design Lines

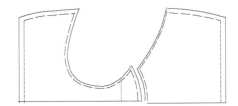
Fitted Briefs Pattern

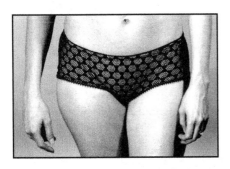

Variations of the Fitted Briefs

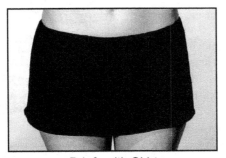

Briefs with Skirt

Briefs with Full Skirt

Fitted Briefs Design Variations

Shown below are five design variations created by changing the location of the
Velcro that indicates the waist and leg openings for a Fitted Briefs.

Mid Scoop Briefs

 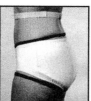  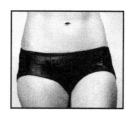 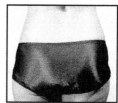

Low Rise Briefs

  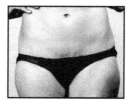 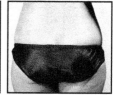

High Rise Briefs

 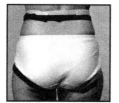  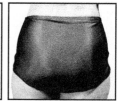

Boy Shorts

High Cut Briefs

   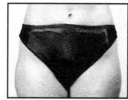 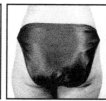

Fitted Briefs Design Process

To create a Fitted Briefs pattern, follow the steps below:
1. Create the design lines using Velcro and bias tape.
2. Measure where the design lines are located on the body.
3. Use the measurements to draw the pattern.
4. Cut the pattern out of scrap fabric and sew a trial Fitted Briefs.

I. Create the Fitted Briefs's Shape

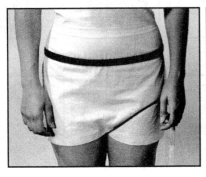 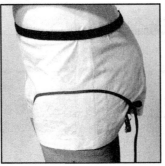 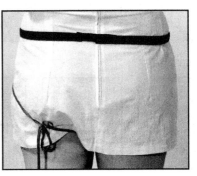

1. Place a strip of Velcro around the body where you want the top of the briefs to be located.
2. Use a length of bias tape to establish the shape of the leg opening.

II. Measure and Draft the Fitted Briefs

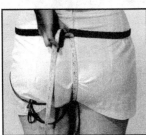

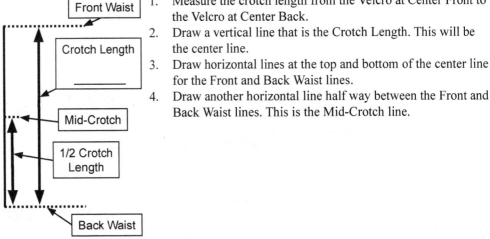

Front Waist

Crotch Length

Mid-Crotch

1/2 Crotch Length

Back Waist

1. Measure the crotch length from the Velcro at Center Front to the Velcro at Center Back.
2. Draw a vertical line that is the Crotch Length. This will be the center line.
3. Draw horizontal lines at the top and bottom of the center line for the Front and Back Waist lines.
4. Draw another horizontal line half way between the Front and Back Waist lines. This is the Mid-Crotch line.

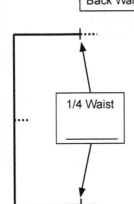

1/4 Waist

5. Measure the distance around the body at the Velcro. This is the Waist measurement.
6. On the Front and Back Waist lines, mark 1/4 of the Waist measurement.

II. Measure and Draft the Fitted Briefs, cont'd

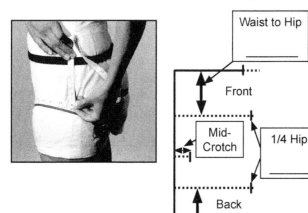

Waist to Hip
_____

Front

Mid-Crotch

1/4 Hip
_____

Back

Waist to Hip

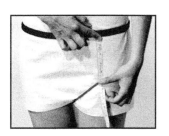

Front of Leg
_____

1/2

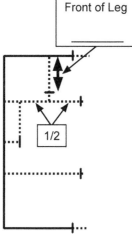

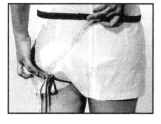

1/2

Step 17

Step 19

Back of Leg
_____

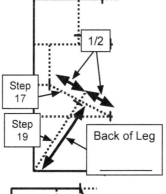

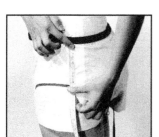

Side Seam
_____

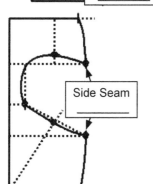

7. For the Hip measurement, measure around the fullest part of the hips.

8. Measure the distance from the Hip Measurement to the Velcro for the waist. This is the Waist to Hip measurement.

9. Use the Waist to Hip measurement to draw horizontal lines for the hip.

10. On the Hip lines, mark 1/4 of the Hip measurement.

11. Use the chart below to mark the length of the Mid-Crotch line.

Hips	Mid-Crotch
Up to 37" (96 cm)	2" (5 cm)
38" to 41" (96 to 104 cm)	2-1/4" (5.7 cm)
Over 41" (104 cm)	2-1/2" (6.4 cm)

12. Measure from the Velcro to the leg bias tape down the front of the leg. This is the Front of Leg length.

13. Draw a line from the end of the Mid-Crotch line up to the Front Hip line.

14. Divide the distance between this line and the side of the Hip line in half, then draw a vertical line. This is the Front of the leg.

15. From the Front Waist line measure down the Front of Leg length and make a mark.

16. Measure the distance from Center Back at the Velcro diagonally to the leg bias tape. This is the Back of Leg length.

17. Draw a diagonal line from the Mid-Crotch line to the end of the Back Hip line.

18. Divide this diagonal line in half and make a mark.

19. Draw a second diagonal line from the Back Waist line through the mark made in Step 18.

20. Mark the Back of Leg length on this second diagonal line.

21. Measure the distance from the Velcro down the side of the body. This is the Side Seam length.

22. Draw dotted lines from the end of the waist to the end of the hip lines, then mark the Side Seam length.

23. Draw the Side Seam.

24. From the Side Seams, draw in the shape of the leg curve.

Fitted Briefs Waist Elastic

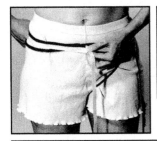

Swimsuit Waist Elastic _____

Plush Waist Elastic _____

The elastic for swimsuits and the plush elastic used for undergarments have different stretch factors. So place the elastic you will be using for the fitted garment around the Velcro indicating the waist line and adjust it for the desired level of comfort, then record the length.

III. Creating a Two-Piece Pattern (optional)

To create a two-piece pattern for Fitted Briefs, follow the steps below.

1. Align your one-piece pattern with the diagram to the right so that it touches the Center and Mid-Crotch lines.
2. Trace the curved hip seam line onto the one-piece pattern.
3. Lay a fresh sheet of paper on top of the one-piece pattern.
4. Trace the front pattern.
5. Slide the paper for the new pattern up 1" (25 mm) to allow for seam allowances.
6. Trace the back pattern.

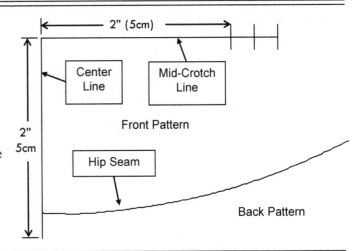

IV. Add Casing and Seam Allowances

Add seam allowances of 3/8" (9 mm) or 1/2" (12 mm) elastic for the waist and 1/4" (6 mm) elastic for the leg openings.

1. Add 1/2" (12 mm) seam allowances to the Side Seams.*
2. Add 1/4" (6 mm) elastic allowances to the leg openings.
3. Add allowances to the front and back waist lines that are the width of the elastic used.
4. For a two-piece pattern, add 1/4" (6 mm) seam allowances to the crotch seams.

*When you create fitted shorts from stretch fabric for swimsuits, baste the fabric together along the Side Seams, then do a trial fitting to determine how snug the Side Seams should be for the wearer.

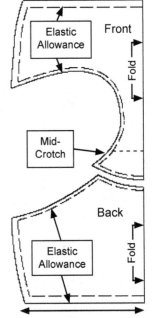

Direction of Greatest Stretch

V. Sewing Fitted Briefs

Briefs made from stretch fabric must be adjusted for the wearer's comfort. The example described here uses stretch fabric, a two-piece pattern, and a lined front panel.

Qty	Materials
2 yds	1/4" (6 mm) Elastic
1	Fabric as required
2 yds	Cording (or shoe laces)

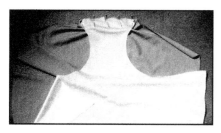

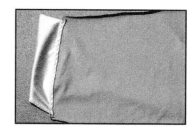

1. Use the pattern to cut out fabric for the Fitted Briefs.
2. Pin the front fashion fabric to the back along the crotch seam, right sides together.
3. Pin the right side of the lining fabric to the wrong side of the back fashion fabric along the crotch seam.
4. Sew the crotch seam with a stretch stitch or 1 mm zigzag stitch.

5. Pin the front lining fabric to the front fashion fabric along the outside edges, wrong sides together, then use a 4 mm zigzag stitch to sew.
6. Pin the Side Seams, right sides together, then machine baste.
7. Verify the fit, adjusting the Side Seam for the fabric as necessary.

8. Sew the Side Seams. Use either a straight stitch, 1 mm zigzag or a stretch stitch according to the vertical stretch of the fabric.
9. Press the Side Seam allowance to the back, then topstitch with either a straight stitch or 2 mm zigzag.

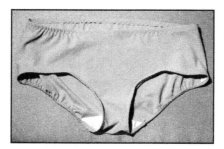

10. Add 1" (25 mm) to the length for the waist elastic already determined in page 46. Then cut the waist elastic to this length.
11. Overlap the elastic ends by 1" (25 mm) and sew together to create a loop of elastic.
12. Pin the loop of waist elastic on the wrong side of the fabric. Stretch the elastic so it is evenly distributed around the briefs's entire waist.
13. Zigzag the elastic to the fashion fabric.
14. Turn the elastic to the inside of

the Fitted Briefs, then zigzag it in place.
15. Cut 1/4" (6 mm) elastic for the leg openings. The elastic should be 1" (25 mm) shorter than the leg opening on the pattern.
16. Overlap the elastic ends by 1" (25 mm) and sew together to create a loop of elastic. The leg elastic is now 2" (5 cm) shorter than the leg opening.
17. Pin the loop of elastic on the wrong side of the fabric, then zigzag the elastic to the fashion fabric. Stretch the elastic while sewing the back half of the briefs.
18. Turn the elastic to the inside of the Fitted Briefs.

Three-Piece Fitted Briefs

Use the pattern on this page to create a three-piece pattern with a separate Crotch Piece.

1. Match the Center and Mid-Crotch lines of the pattern below to your pattern.
2. Copy the appropriate front and back crotch seams to the Fitted Shorts pattern. These seams do not change the shape of the Fitted Shorts.
3. Adjust the shape of the leg opening's seam for fit as necessary.
4. Trace the three pattern pieces onto separate sheets of pattern paper.
5. Add seam allowances to the waist, Side Seam, leg, and crotch seams.

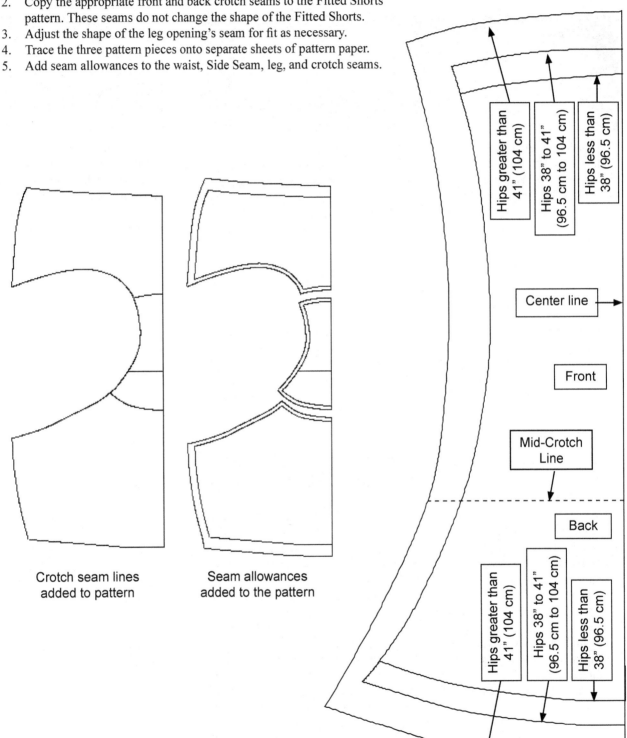

Crotch seam lines
added to pattern

Seam allowances
added to the pattern

Fitted Skirt Pattern for Briefs

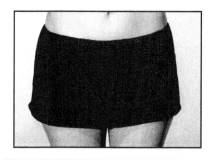

Skirts can be added to Fitted Briefs by draping muslin as illustrated. The resulting skirt can either have some fullness or follow the lines of the body fairly closely. You can either use a waistband or join the skirt to the top of the shorts. For the fitted look, use stretch fabric so the shorts and skirt can be pulled over the hips.

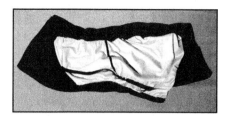

Sew skirt to briefs at waist

Drape a Fitted Skirt

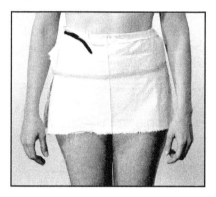

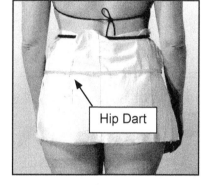

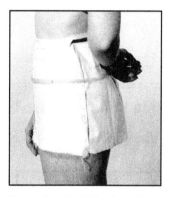

1. Sew vertical lines of black stay stitching on two rectangles of muslin.
2. Secure the muslin to the natural waist with Velcro and pins.
3. Adjust the Center Front line so it is at the center of the body and vertical to the floor.

4. Adjust the Center Back line so it is at the center of the body and vertical to the floor.
5. To create a fitted skirt, pin in a hip dart. Use two cross-hatched pins (+) to indicate the point of the dart and another pin at the waist for the width of the dart.

6. Determine the Side Seam by folding the front muslin where you want the Side Seam to be located, then pin in place.
7. Place a second line of Velcro around the body where the top of the Fitted Briefs is located, then mark the waist.

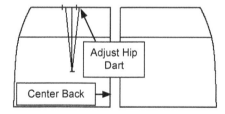

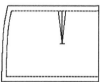 

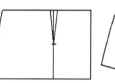 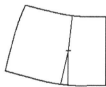

8. Copy the lines from the muslin to a paper pattern.
9. Draw a center line from the point of the dart to the waist that is parallel to the Center Back line.
10. Adjust the width of the dart so it is centered over the dart center line.
11. Draw the sides of the dart.

12. On a second piece of pattern paper, trace the lines for the skirt, then add seam allowances.

Alternately, you can remove the dart which allows the fabric to drape off the hip.
1. Make a copy of the back pattern.
2. Draw a line from the point of the dart down to the hip parallel to Center Back, then cut along this line.
3. Cut out the dart shape, then tape the pattern together at the dart.
4. Smooth out the waist and hem lines.

Adding Fullness to Skirt Patterns

The pattern design technique for adding fullness to a garment is useful for a variety of looks. The design on the left adds fullness to the hem but not the waist. The design on the right adds gathering at the waist.

The instructions below show how to add fullness by tracing an existing pattern.

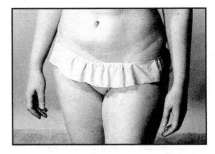

This design uses an elasticized waistband sewn on after skirt and briefs are zigzagged together.

The hem is finished with decorative neckline elastic.

This design adds ruffles at the waist with the elastic waistband turned under and sewn to the briefs but not the ruffle.

The hem of the ruffle is cut with a hot knife and uses no other finishing technique.

Adding Fullness to the Hem of a Pattern

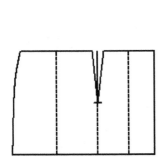

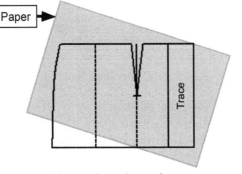

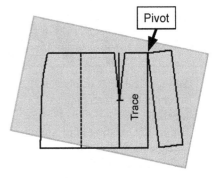

1. Draw slash lines on a copy of the fitted patterns as illustrated. One slash line should be drawn down from the point of the dart.

2. Place a clean sheet of pattern paper on top of the original pattern.
3. Trace the first rectangle from the Center Back line to the first slash line.

4. Pivot the pattern at the top of the first slash line.
5. Trace the pattern from the first slash line to the dart and down the second slash line.

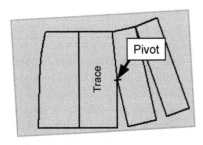

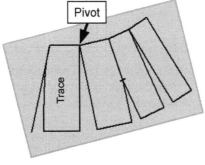

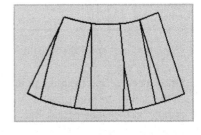

6. Pivot the pattern at the point of the dart to close the dart shape.
7. Trace from the dart to the third slash line.

8. Pivot the pattern at the top of the third slash line.
9. Trace the third slash line and the waist and hem to the Side Seam.
10. Draw a straight Side Seam down from the waist.

11. Smooth out the curve of the waist and hem lines.
12. Add seam allowances, then follow the same procedure with the front pattern.

Bandeau Tops & Dresses

A Bandeau Top is usually a straight rectangle of fabric snug to the above the bust circumference at its top edge and the rib cage at its bottom. The descriptions here show how to make a Bandeau Top that has a horizontal dart from Center Front to the Apex, thus creating a more flattering shape.

For this style, use Velcro to indicate the design lines on the wearer. To create the pattern, you can then measure from key reference points to the design lines. This style usually requires a little additional fitting to optimize the shaping. Foam may be added to the front lining.

The Bandeau Top pattern can be used for diverse designs, including:
- Bandeau Bra
- Strapless Bandeau Tops
- Bandeau Tops with Cording
- Ring Bandeau Tops

Adding a skirt below the rib cage can also expand a Bandeau pattern for a short top, dress, or full length gown.

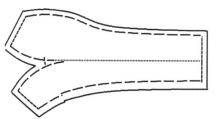

Bandeau Bra

Strapless Bandeau

Bandeau with Straps

Bandeau Top

Bandeau Dress

Bandeau Gown

The Bandeau Top Design Process

To create a Bandeau Top, follow the steps below:
1. Create the shape for the Bandeau Top.
2. Measure then draw the Bandeau Top.
3. Shape the Bandeau.
4. Fit a trial muslin top.

I. Create the Shape for the Bandeau Top

1. Define the top of the Bandeau by securing a strip of Velcro above the bust.
2. Define the bottom of the Bandeau by securing a second strip of Velcro around the rib cage.

> **Note:** To allow room for adjustments during fitting, measure to the outside edges of the Velcro.
>
> For breasts that are not self supporting, measurements may be taken over an existing bra. Ideally, the Full Bust should be approximately half way between the Above Bust and the Rib Cage. This would make the "Top to Apex" and "Apex to Rib Cage" approximately equal. If this does not provide appropriate support for the breasts, you may adjust the measurements so the "Top to Apex" is no more than 1/2" (12 mm) greater than the "Apex to Rib Cage" measurement.

II. Measure then Draw the Bandeau Top

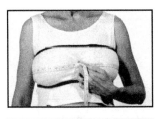
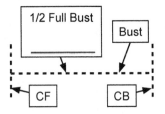

1. Measure the circumference at the fullest part of the bust.
2. Draw a horizontal line that is 1/2 the length of the Full Bust measurement. This is the Bust line.
3. For the Center Front (CF) and Center Back (CB) lines, draw vertical lines at either end of the Bust line.

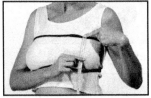
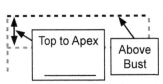

4. Measure the distance from the top Velcro to the Apex.
5. On the Center Front line, mark the Top to Apex length.
6. Draw a horizontal line from this mark. This is the Above Bust line.

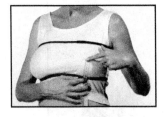
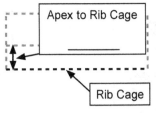

7. Measure the distance from the Apex to the bottom Velcro.
8. On the Center Front line, mark the Apex to Rib Cage length.
9. Draw a horizontal line from this mark. This is the Rib Cage line.

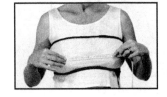
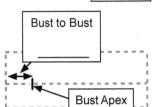

10. Measure the distance from Bust Apex to Bust Apex.
11. Measure 1/2 the Bust to Bust length from Center Front and make a mark. This is the Bust Apex point.

II. Measure then Draw the Bandeau, cont'd

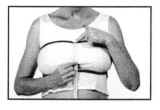

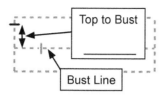

Top to Bust

_____

Bust Line

12. At Center Front, measure from the top Velcro to the full bust.
13. On the pattern, measure up this distance from the Bust line and make a mark.

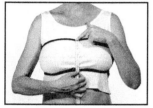

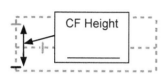

CF Height

_____

14. At Center Front, measure from the top Velcro to the bottom Velcro, then mark this length on the pattern.

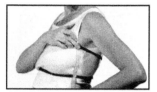

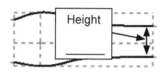

Height

_____

15. Along the side of the body, measure the distance between the top and bottom Velcro. This will be the Center Back height of the Bandeau.
16. Mark half the height above the full bust line and half below.
17. Using the marks at Center Front, Apex, and Center Back as guides, draw in the shape of the Bandeau.

III. Shape the Bandeau

For shaping, the Bandeau needs to be adjusted to the dimensions of the body.

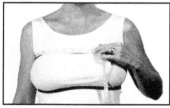

1. Record the 1/2 Bust measurement from page 52 in the chart below.
2. Inhale and measure the Above the Bust circumference, then record half this measurement in the chart below.
3. Subtract the Above Bust measurement from the Bust measurement and record below.

1/2 Bust: _____	Minus	1/2 Above Bust: _____	Equals: _____

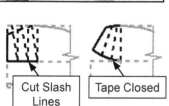

Cut Slash Lines

Tape Closed

4. Use the difference to draw slash lines to establish how much the top of the Bandeau must be reduced. For example, if the difference is 1-1/2" (36 mm), draw 3 slash lines to remove 1/2" (12 mm) each.
5. Cut the pattern along the bust and slash lines, then tape it closed.

6. Record the 1/2 Bust measurement in the chart below.
7. Inhale and measure the Rib Cage circumference, then record half this measurement in the chart below.
8. Subtract the Rib Cage measurement from the Bust measurement and record below.

1/2 Bust: _____	Minus	1/2 Rib Cage: _____	Equals: _____

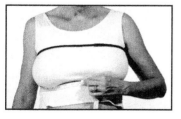

Cut Slash Lines

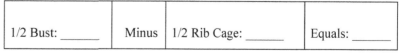

Tape Closed

9. Use the difference to draw slash lines to establish how much the top of the Bandeau must be reduced. For example, if the difference is 1-1/2", (36 mm) draw 3 slash lines to remove 1/2" (12 mm) each.
10. Cut the pattern along the slash lines, then tape it closed.

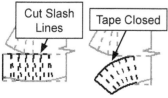

IV. Measure Elastic for the Bandeau

For the top and bottom of the Bandeau, hold elastic around the body and adjust it to the wearer's comfort level, then record the length.

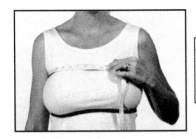

Above Bust Elastic

_____

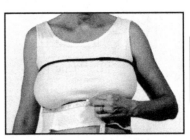

Rib Cage Elastic

_____

V. Fit a Trial Muslin Bandeau Top

To finalize the pattern shape, the Bandeau Top should be carefully fitted.

1. Add 1/4" (6 mm) seam allowance to the pattern's horizontal dart.
2. Add 3/4" (2 cm) seam allowances to the remainder of the pattern.
3. Cut two copies of the Bandeau out of scrap fabric.
4. Sew the darts closed and press down.
5. Pin the two halves of the Bandeau along the Center Front seam, right sides together, then sew.
6. Press the Center Front seam open.
7. For a trial fitting, pin the Center Back closed on the wearer.
8. Pin additional darts as necessary to optimize fit.
9. Place Velcro around the body above the bust and at the rib cage, then draw lines on the muslin.
10. Remove the Bandeau and adjust the pattern as necessary.

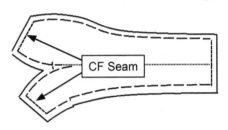

CF Seam

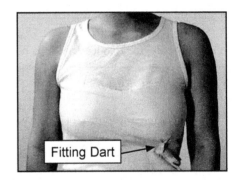

Fitting Dart

VI. Adjust the Pattern After Fitting

- Expand or reduce the size of the Center Front dart as necessary.
- Darts added to adjust the fit to the Above Bust or Rib Cage seam show how much the slash lines need to be increased or reduced. If necessary, the point of a dart can be extended past the Apex to the side of the Bandeau.
- Adjust the Above Bust and Rib Cage seams and Center Back position as necessary.

Basic Bandeau Top

I. Adjust the Seam and Elastic Allowance

The sewing instructions that follow are for a Bandeau made from a stretch fabric, its edges finished with plush elastic for underwear. For light weight fabric such as tricot, use a second lining fabric.

1. Add seam allowances to the top and bottom edges that are the width of the plush elastic.
2. Add 1/2" (12 mm) seam allowances to all other edges.
3. Pin the pattern to fabric and cut. The direction of greatest stretch should be around the body.

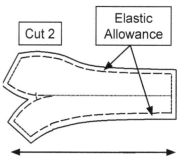

Direction of Greatest Stretch

II. Sew the Bandeau Top

1. If you are using a double layer of fabric, zigzag the two layers together around the outside edges.
2. Sew the darts closed with a stretch stitch.
3. Press the darts toward the bottom and topstitch with a small zigzag.
4. From the inside, trim the darts close to the topstitching.
5. Pin the Center Front seam closed, then sew using a stretch stitch.
6. Press open the Center Front seam and topstitch the seam allowances.
7. From the inside, trim the seam allowances close to the topstitching.
8. Determine the length for the top elastic by wrapping it around the body above the bust, stretching for the fit desired.
9. Turn the Bandeau good side out.
10. Place the elastic on the top edge of the Bandeau with the soft side up. The picot edge should be facing the body of the Bandeau.
11. Pin the elastic to the Bandeau. The elastic's outside edge should follow the outside of the seam allowance.
12. To sew the picot edge to the Bandeau, use a small narrow zigzag. The stitching should be as close to the edge of the elastic as possible without going over the edge.
13. Trim the seam allowance.
14. Turn the elastic to the inside of the Bandeau.
15. Hand baste the elastic so the picot edge is exposed along the top edge of the Bandeau.
16. To finish the elastic installation, sew a three-step zigzag or serpentine stitch. This line of stitching should follow the edge of the elastic that is opposite the small zigzag sewn in Step 12.
17. Remove the basting.
18. Determine the length of the bottom elastic by wrapping it around the body at the rib cage, stretching for the fit desired.
19. To sew the bottom elastic, follow the procedures described in Steps 9 through 17.
20. Pin the Center Back seam closed, then sew using a stretch stitch.
21. Press open the Center Back seam and topstitch the seam allowances.
22. From the inside, trim the seam allowances close to the topstitching.

Qty	Materials
3 yds	1/2" (12 mm) Elastic
1	Fabric as required

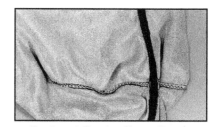

Dart and Center Front Seam

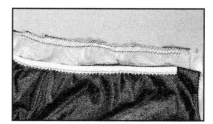

1st Plush Elastic Zigzag

Basting and 2nd Zigzag

55

Bandeau With Skirt

The Bandeau pattern can be combined with a skirt to make tops, dresses, and gowns. The procedure is the same as for creating a skirt for a Bikini Top, see page 27.

When the garment is made from stretch fabric, there is no need for an opening device, such as a zipper, at Center Back. This means both Center Back and Center Front will be on a fold.

The use of foam to stabilize the Bandeau's shape is optional. This example includes instructions for how to add it.

I. The Skirt Pattern

Create a skirt pattern as described on page 27. One design option is for the Bandeau to be gathered at Center Front. The photo shows how this changes the top of the front of the skirt. There should be a minimum of 2" (5 cm) of ease at the hips.

1. On a copy of the skirt pattern, extend the hem to the desired length.
2. Verify the amount of ease at the hip.
3. Add 1/2" (12 mm) seam and hem allowances to the sides and bottom.
4. Add the width of the rib cage elastic to the top of the skirt pattern.
5. To cut two pieces of foam for the front, use the Bandeau pattern with no seam allowances.
6. To cut the top from both the fashion fabric and the lining, use the Bandeau pattern.
7. To cut a front and back skirt, use the skirt pattern. Notch the Center Front.

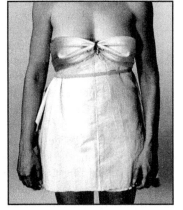

Gathered Top

II. Sew the Skirt

Sew the Side Seams of the skirt together. The skirt may be hemmed at this point or as a final step after the entire garment is together. These instructions are for a garment made out of stretch fabric.

1. Pin the Side Seams of the skirt, right sides together, then sew with a 1 mm zigzag.
2. Press the Side Seams to the back.
3. Topstitch the seam allowance to the body of the skirt using a 2 mm zigzag.
4. Trim off the excess seam allowance.
5. Use a long straight stitch to machine baste the hem length desired.
6. Along the basting, press the hem under, then topstitch using a zigzag stitch.
7. Remove the basting.

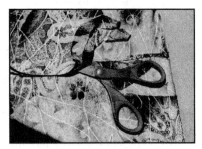

Trimming Seam Allowance

III. Sew the Top

The first step is to sew the foam into the lining. The fashion fabric is then sewn and combined with the lining. When sewing the elastic, don't put too much stretch in the front where the foam is located. Stretch the elastic mostly in the back.

1. Pin the foam to the lining, then sew using a 4 mm zigzag stitch.

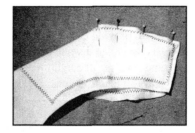

2. Pin the dart along the edge of the foam, then sew.

3. Press the dart allowance to the bottom, then topstitch in place with a 2 mm zigzag stitch.
4. Trim off the excess dart allowance.

5. Pin the Center Front closed, then sew. You can use a straight stitch for this seam.
6. Press the Center Front seam allowance open, then topstitch in place.
7. Trim off the excess fabric from the Center Front seam allowances.
8. To sew the fashion fabric, repeat Steps 2 through 7.

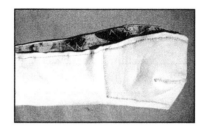

9. Pin the lining to the fashion fabric, wrong sides together, along the top of the Bandeau.
10. Using a 4 mm zigzag stitch, zigzag the fashion fabric to the lining.
11. Using the measurement for the Above Bust on page 54 plus 1" (25 mm), cut a length of elastic.
12. Zigzag the elastic into a loop by overlapping it 1" (25 mm).
13. Pin the elastic to the elastic allowance along the top of the Bandeau.
14. Using a 4 mm zigzag stretch, sew the elastic to the top. These stitches should be along the edge of the elastic furthest from the top's edge.

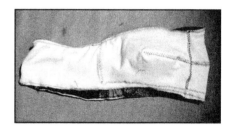

15. Hand baste the top edge of the Bandeau so that the edge of the lining is hidden behind the fashion fabric.
16. Zigzag the top edge of the Bandeau.
17. Remove the basting.
18. Pin the fashion fabric to the lining along the bottom of the Bandeau Top, then sew using a 4 mm zigzag stitch.

IV. Sew the Top to the Skirt

The top and the skirt can now be combined.

1. Pin the skirt to the top along the rib cage seam, good sides together, then sew using a stretch stitch or a 1 mm+ zigzag.
2. Using a 4 mm zigzag, sew the rib cage seam allowances together.
3. Using the Rib Cage measurement from page 54 plus 1" (25 mm), cut a length of elastic.
4. Using a 4 mm zigzag, sew the elastic in a loop.
5. Pin the elastic to the rib cage seam allowance, then sew with a 4 mm zigzag close to the seam at the rib cage.
6. Press the seam allowance down, then topstitch in place.

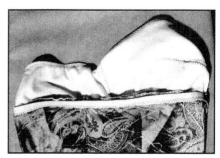

Rib Cage Elastic

Bust Sling Bras

The Bust Sling Bra is designed to provide comfortable support regardless of cup size. Bust Sling patterns can be used to create diverse under and outer garments which have built-in support structure so no separate undergarment is required. Outer garments include Swimsuit Tops, dresses, and full length gowns.

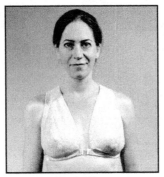

Basic Bra

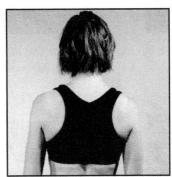

Racerback Bra

Zipper Opening

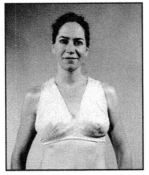

Hybrid Bras

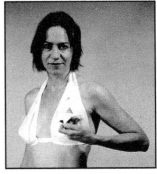

Nursing Bras

Swimsuit Tops

Dresses

Gowns

Structure of the Bust Sling Bra

Conventional bras are based on a cantilever concept: The weight of the breast is supported by a band around the rib cage. The Bust Sling Bra changes the support structure to a suspension style that follows the natural contours of the body, eliminating the need for an undergarment. This approach also eliminates the need for underwires. It is an open design concept that can be used to create garments for women regardless of age or degree of support needed.

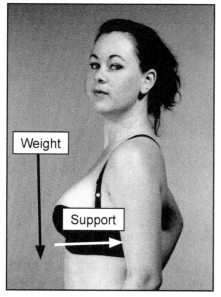
Conventional Cantilever Support

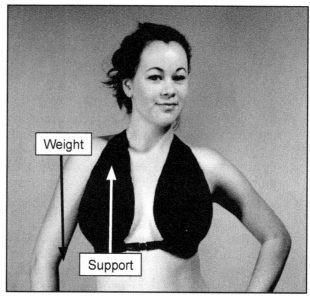
Bust Sling Suspension Support

An additional feature of the Bust Sling Bra is that the straps can be adjusted to individual needs and designs. The instructions in this book are for diverse strap widths and the back support options shown below.

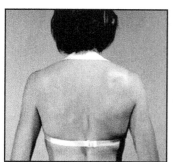
Halter Back

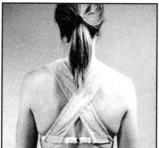
X-Back

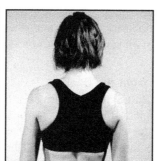
Racerback

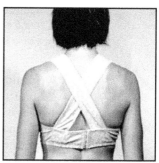
Hybrid Hook & Eye

Bra Design Issues

Underwires

A conventional bra uses an underwire to hold the bra cup close to the body, particularly at the breast bone. Bra underwires can be problematic because:

- Incorrect lengths poke the underarm area.
- The left and right breasts can be different sizes.
- Some women need an underwire that is flat on the bottom and no commercial underwire is shaped like this.
- With time, underwires ultimately poke through channeling.

The Bust Sling Bra eliminates the need for an underwire by using a suspension structure that follows the natural contours of the body.

Separation between Breasts

Some women have no separation between the breasts at the full bust level. This means that the underwires of a conventional bra cannot go high enough to provide adequate control of the breast tissue. The Bust Sling bra only requires the thickness of the fabric to fit between the breasts to provide appropriate support. Moreover, fabric between the breasts absorbs perspiration.

Front Opening

The largest front closure clasp for a conventional bra is 1-3/8" (35 mm), which is inadequate for preventing East/West drift. The Bust Sling Bra removes the tension around the rib cage, allowing for a variety of front closure devices including separating zippers. This is especially convenient for women who find it difficult to manipulate a bra's back closure.

Bra Strap Width

The largest readily available width for a conventional bra strap is 3/4" (2 cm). A narrow bra strap can pinch nerves and result in other serious health issues. The width of the strap for Bust Sling Bras can be up to the full width of the shoulder–even wider than that found on backpacks. For women whose breasts are smaller or self supporting, the straps on a Bust Sling can be as narrow as 1/8" (3 mm).

Support from the Back

Since the Bust Sling Bra relies on suspension, support from the back up to the shoulders is important. As with strap width, this varies for individuals. For this reason, the book includes a halter style around the neck, an X-Back, a racer back, and a hybrid that uses the same kind of band around the rib cage as a conventional bra.

East/West Drift

Large breasts tend to spread to the sides. The Bust Sling Bra uses two means for controlling this East/West drift. The position of a Bust Sling's two sides can be adjusted at the rib cage. Additional support can be added to the full bust level with a bridge between the two Bust Slings. This bridge can incorporate a zipper. If desired, the bridge can even be carried above the full bust level.

Rib Cage Elastic

With conventional bras, the elastic band under the bust can roll up and become uncomfortable. For the Bust Sling Bra, elastic of any width can be used, including the wide non-roll elastic used in waistbands. Some women may not even need elastic. This can be an important consideration for women who have scar tissue from surgery.

Life Expectancy of the Bra

Many women find a bra's elastic loses tension after only three or four months, rendering the bra unusable. The structure of a Bust Sling Bra is such that it does not depend on tension. As mentioned above, it may even be possible to make a Bust Sling garment with no elastic. This means a Bust Sling Bra should have long life expectancy.

Support for Fluff

Soft tissue around the rib cage is known as "fluff." This is uncomfortable when pinched by a tight band around the rib cage. With the Bust Sling Bra, support comes over the shoulders, minimizing the tension around the rib cage. In addition, by offering different styles for the back, such as the racer back and the hybrid, there is built-in support for this fluff.

Profile Enhancement

The Bust Sling can include a pocket for either one side or both, allowing the insertion of a foam bra cup for profile enhancement or a prosthetic device.

Styling Concerns

Conventional bras for large breasts are often plain. Bust Sling Bras can be made with any type of fabric and any type of elastic. So long as the underlying structure is maintained, the lines can be changed to create different designs. Furthermore, the structure of the Bust Sling can be used to create Empire style tops, dresses, and gowns that do not require an additional undergarment.

Bust Sling Nursing Bra

One of the most sensitive times for a woman's breasts is when she becomes pregnant and then starts nursing. The Bust Sling Bra is particularly well suited to be a nursing bra.

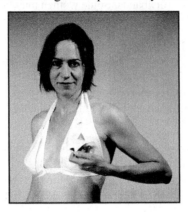

Among the first women to create and use a Bust Sling Nursing Bra was Kenna, who wears a "DDD" cup in a conventional bra, was new to sewing, and yet found this an easy garment to make. With her permission, I have included her comments below. She is not the model you see in the photo above.

Bust Sling vs. Conventional Bra

"For nursing, the bra works very well. I have quite a bit of experience with conventional nursing bras. Usually the part of the bra that falls away for nursing is the part of the bra that supports the breast. Therefore, when you nurse, the bra drops the breast. I love the fact that the bust sling does not do that. The breast is supported through the nursing, and that feels better to me. I do have to hold my baby a little further out from my body due to the projection, but that has not been a problem."

Fungal Growth

"It's not unusual for women with ample busts to struggle with fungal growth on the skin underneath the breast. This is a real problem. The Bust Sling design prevents skin-on-skin contact, which prevents sweating, which prevents that fungal growth. A+ for the help in that department."

Mastitis

"The other day I started experiencing pain from a clogged milk duct. Guess what! The fact that the Bust Sling Bra has no underwire and is very gentle on the breast tissue made it the perfect bra to wear while trying to prevent the pain from turning into full-blown mastitis. Another A+."

Cost and Durability

"I love the cost factor. When I buy conventional bras, they easily cost me $60.00 per bra, if not more. Then they last for no more than a year, and often times less than that. If I launder them adequately to prevent fungal growth, they will last no more than 3 months. [Now] I can make a bra out of material that can be laundered, and I can do it very economically."

Basic Bust Sling Bra

The basic Bust Sling Bra pattern is the foundation for all the other styles.

Parts of the Bust Sling Bra

The Bust Sling Band is shaped around the breast from the outside to the underside, then the inside, up, and over the back. It can be cut from a single piece of woven material. This single band is the weight bearing structure of the bra.

The Styling Cup, shaped like a drop of water, is added last to the mold and can control the projection of the breast but should not be weight bearing. For most women, it is a three-dimensional shape that needs a dart or seam to create a flat pattern.

The Rib Cage Elastic is the elastic that holds the Bust Sling in place. It should fit snugly around the rib cage but does not need to be tight because it is not weight bearing. The elastic is attached to the Bust Sling Band using a casing. The Rib Cage Elastic can either be pulled over the head or have a closing device.

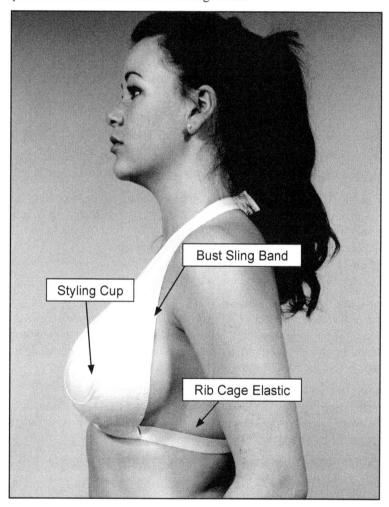

Materials and Supplies

Supplies for making Bust Sling Bras can be divided into two categories: supplies required for muslin mock-ups and supplies for finished garments. Note: for finished garments, you can use virtually any kind of garment-appropriate fabric and some form of elastic at the rib cage to accommodate breathing.

To create the initial Bust Sling mold, the technique I have found most efficient utilizes Glad's Press'n Seal which is applied directly to the skin to shape and support the breast, then reinforced with masking tape before removal.

The pattern should be recorded on pattern paper. It is a good idea to do a trial test of the pattern shapes using posterboard. The patterns are then cut out of muslin for a trial fitting. For this fitting, use elastic around the rib cage. The muslin trial can either be pulled over the head or a G-Hook can be used to open the bra at Center Front.

Qty	Item
1 roll	Glad Press'n Seal
1 each	Masking tape, 3/4" & 2"
1	Marking Pen (i.e. Sharpie)
1	Posterboard
1	Pattern paper
1	Muslin
1 yd	Elastic, 3/4" or 5/8"
1	G-Hook (optional)
3	Bra Strap Sliders (optional)

The Pattern Design Process

There are three basic steps for creating custom-fit patterns for Bust Sling Bras. Instructions are provided so you can either do-it-yourself or do it with the help of a second person.

1. Create a mold using Press'n Seal and masking tape.
2. Convert the mold into paper patterns.
3. Create a muslin mock-up and verify the fit.

Using Press'n Seal to Create a Mold

Press'n Seal creates a protective layer on the body that can then be covered with masking tape. The masking tape stabilizes the mold and can be used to enhance the shaping. Once the shape is achieved, the design lines desired can be drawn directly on the masking tape before the mold is removed from the body.

Shaping the Styling Cup

Once the Bust Sling Band has been created to support the breast tissue, the Styling Cup can be added. The Styling Cup can either be designed to create maximum projection or to compress the breast tissue for minimum projection.

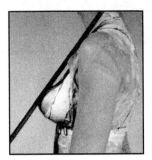
Open Cup

Compressed Cup

Create the Bust Sling Mold

The instructions shown here are for a two-person operation. To create a mold as a do-it-yourself process, see page 66.

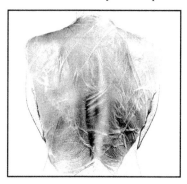

1. Apply a wide sheet of Press'n Seal to cover the full back.

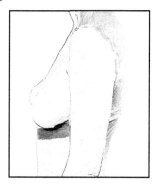

2. Apply a strip of Press'n Seal around the rib cage just under the bust.

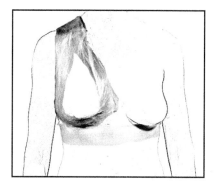

3. Apply a strip of Press'n Seal from the shoulder down along the side of the breast, under the bust, then along the inside of the breast back up to the shoulder.

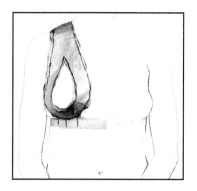

4. Use the masking tape to stabilize the shape of the Press'n Seal.
5. Draw in the front design lines for the Bust Sling Band.
6. On the Rib Cage Band, mark the location where the Bust Sling Band joins the Rib Cage Band and the Apex of the breast.

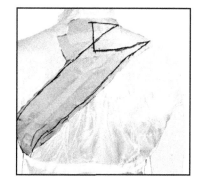

7. Apply masking tape across the back from the top of the Bust Sling Band to the side of the other breast.
8. Hold a string around the neck and draw in the back of the neck.
9. Draw in the location of the Center Back following the spinal column.

10. Draw two lines from the top of the shoulder at the neck down to the rib cage near the outside of the breast on the opposite side of the body.

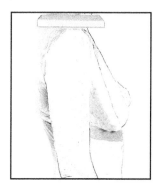

11. To determine the shoulder seam, place a book on top of the shoulder, then mark this location on the mold.

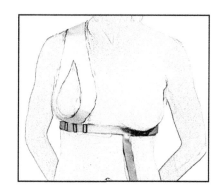

12. Use a length of elastic to determine the tension desired for the rib cage elastic.

13. Use Press'n Seal to add the Styling Cup to the front of the bra.

Create a Do-It-Yourself Bust Sling Mold

To create a mold as a single-person operation, the concept is the same as described on page 65, but it is easier to follow a slightly different sequence.

Note: As a do-it-yourself process, I recommend starting with an open cup shape and adding the Styling Cup later in the process.

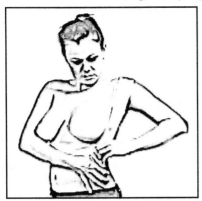 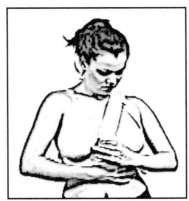 

1. Cut several strips of Press'n Seal about 2 yards long, then cover with masking tape.
2. Wrap one strip of Press'n Seal around the front of the rib cage from one side to the other, around the back, over the shoulder, and back to the end of the strip where you started.
3. Use a second strip to go around the body as in Step 2, but pull it down from the shoulder on the inside of the breast and anchor it at the rib cage.
4. Use a third strip around the rib cage to secure the first two strips.
5. To lift the breast, use a shorter strip starting under the breast and attach its ends to the strips from Steps 2 and 3. Tape it securely in place.
6. Use a short strip to secure the strip from Step 5 to the rib cage.
7. Add whatever tape is required to hold the strips securely in place, then remove the mold and proceed to creating a pattern for an open cup Bust Sling Bra.

Create the Paper Pattern

The Bust Sling Mold captures the shape of the body. This needs to be converted into a paper pattern by first testing the shape with poster board, then creating the paper pattern. For the initial fitting, I recommend doing an open cup bra so that you are only fitting the Bust Sling Band. Once this shape is established, you can add the Styling Cup.

I. Copy the Mold to Posterboard

Note: Since the shape of the Bust Sling varies with each body, the one you make may or may not look the same as what is shown in these illustrations.

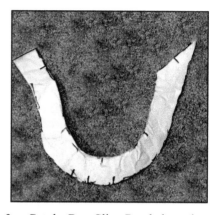

1. Immediately after the Bust Sling mold is removed from the body, reinforce the shape with masking tape on the inside of the mold.

2. Verify the design lines. There will be a seam where the inside of the Bust Sling Band is attached to the outside of the band. Use a sewing notch to indicate where they join.

3. Cut the Bust Sling Band along the design lines.
4. Cut the front of the Bust Sling Band from the back at the shoulder seam.

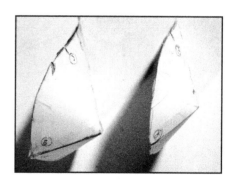

5. Trace the Press'n Seal mold onto the posterboard.
6. Cut the posterboard along the sewing lines.
7. Tape the poster board together, then verify the fit by holding it up to the body.

8. Determine the location of the apex of the bust on the Styling Cup.
9. Cut from the bottom of the Styling Cup to the apex.
10. Trace the Styling Cup mold onto posterboard.
11. Tape the posterboard Styling Cup to the Bust Sling Band.

Above are two different Styling Cups for the same body. The mold for the left is made for maximum projection. The one on the right is made for minimum projection.

II. Create the Paper Pattern

The posterboard pattern verifies accuracy. Now the shapes from the posterboard must be traced onto pattern paper so seam allowances can be added for cutting a trial muslin.

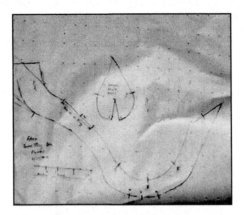

1. Trace the posterboard shapes for the back of the Bust Sling Band onto pattern paper. Use the dots on the paper to establish the straight of the goods.
2. Transfer the sewing notches with their numbers to the posterboard.
3. To create the casing for the rib cage elastic, draw a rectangle that is the length between the sewing notches marked on the Bust Sling Band.
4. On the pattern for the rib cage elastic, draw a line to indicate the true bias at a 45 degree angle from the edge of the pattern.
5. Add 1/4" (6 mm) seam allowances to all seams.

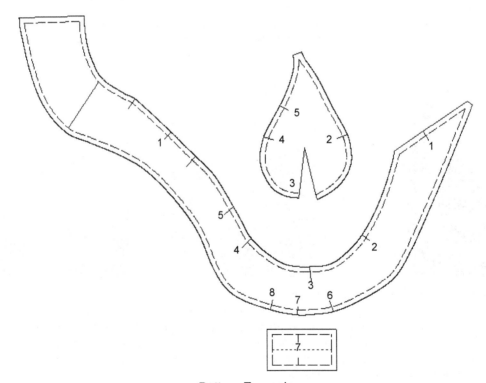

Pattern Example

Create and Fit a Muslin Mock-Up

To verify the fit of the Bust Sling Bra patterns, do a first fitting with an open cup bra. This will ensure the shape of the band is correct. Once the band is shaped correctly, you can add the Styling Cup for a second fitting.

1. Sew an Open Cup Muslin Mock Up.
2. Fit the Open Cup Bust Sling.
3. Adjust the Paper Pattern.
4. Sew for a Second Fitting.
5. Do the Second Fitting.

I. Sew an Open Cup Muslin Mock Up

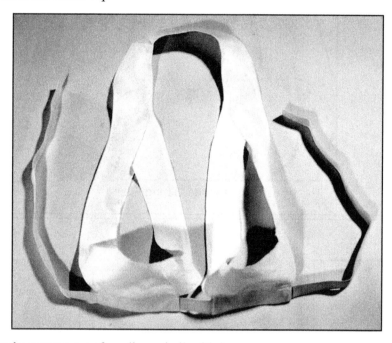

1. Cut the patterns out of muslin or similar fabric.
2. Mark the sewing notches.
3. Pin the Bust Sling Bands at the vertical seam that joins the inside of the band to its outside. Create one for each breast.
4. Sew the vertical seam that joins the inside of the Bust Sling Band to the outside.
5. Sew the halter neck at Center Back.
6. Turn under the elastic casings' ends and zigzag in place.
7. Pin the elastic casing to the bottom of the Bust Sling Band, good sides together.
8. Use a 1/4" (6 mm) seam allowance to sew a line of stay stitching around the outside edges of the Bust Sling Band, including the elastic casing.
9. Press under the outside edges.
10. To secure the seam allowance to the wrong side of the Bust Sling Band, zigzag around the outside edges. As you sew, pull the elastic casing away from the bottom of the Bust Sling Band so the zigzag only sews through the seam allowances of the elastic casing.
11. Alternatively, you can zigzag 3 bra strap sliders to each of the two elastic casings.
12. Thread elastic through the elastic casing or the bra strap sliders.

II. Fit the Open Cup Bust Sling

Fit the open cup muslin Bust Sling so that the Bust Sling Bands are snug against the body, adjusting the soft tissue of the breast as necessary. Pin any fittings so they cross from the outside edge of the Bust Sling Band to the inside edge. The example below uses a muslin mock-up that has been deliberately changed to illustrate fitting issues that may arise.

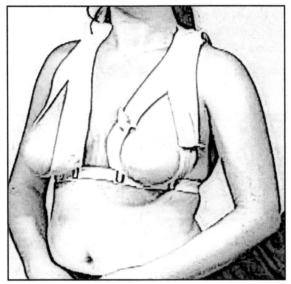

Bust Sling Pinned During Fitting

III. Adjust the Paper Pattern

  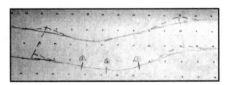

1. Mark the position of the pins from the fitting. Be sure to mark both sides of the pin locations.

2. Copy the fitting marks from the muslin to the paper pattern.
3. Use the fitting marks to draw solid lines from the inside edge of the Bust Sling Band to the outside edge.
4. Mark an "X" on the portions of the pattern to be removed.
5. Cut along one edge of each fitting adjustment, then match the cut edge to the opposite side.

6. Tape the fitting adjustment closed.
7. Copy the pattern onto a fresh sheet of pattern paper, adjusting any areas that are uneven as you go.
8. Add 1/4" (6 mm) seam allowances to the new pattern.

IV. Sew for a Second Fitting

For the final fitting, sew the Styling Cups into the Bust Slings with one Bust Sling for each breast. Each of the images below shows the initial part of a process on the left, with the finished results on the right.

 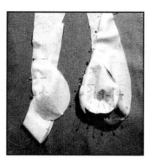 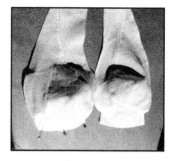

1. Use tracing paper to trace the Styling Cup darts to the muslin.
2. Pin, then sew the darts.
3. Press the dart allowance to the outside of the Styling Cup.
4. Zigzag along the dart allowance.
5. Trim off the excess dart allowance.
6. Pin the top of the Styling Cup to the inside of the Bust Sling Band.
7. Sew a short length of the Styling Cup to the inside of the Bust Sling Band.
8. Pin the remainder of the Styling Cup to the Bust Sling Band.
9. Pin the vertical seam of the Bust Sling Band.
10. Sew the Bust Sling Band to the Styling Cup. Keep the Styling Cup down on the sewing machine with the band up. This allows you to adjust the fabric of the band as you sew the seam, preventing puckering.
11. Use a 1/4" (6 mm) seam allowance to sew stay stitching along the ends of the elastic casings.
12. Fold the seam allowance under, then zigzag in place.
13. Fold the elastic casing in half lengthwise, then pin to the bottom of the Bust Sling at the sewing notches, right sides together.
14. Sew the elastic casing to the Bust Sling.
15. Pin, then sew the back of the Bust Sling to the front at Center Back.
16. Use a 3 mm zigzag stitch to sew 1/4" (6 mm) elastic around the outside edge of the Bust Sling.
17. Turn the elastic to the inside and zigzag in place.
18. Thread elastic through the elastic casing or the bra strap sliders.

Bust Sling Muslin Mock-Up

V. The Second Fitting

Verify the fit of the Bust Sling with the addition of the Styling Cup.

During this fitting, you can drape a piece of muslin at Center Front to create a bridge up to the full bust level. This bridge can be used to control the East/West drift of the breasts.

Another area for which you can provide additional coverage is the side of the Bust Sling. Drape a piece of muslin on the side to control fluff in this area.

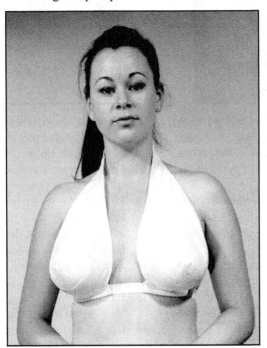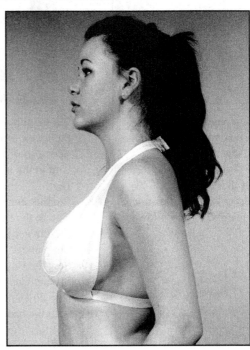

The Finished Muslin Mock-Up

Bust Sling Bra Variations

This chapter describes three enhancements for shaping Bust Sling Bras. For larger breasts, using two bands can enhance shaping by reducing the projection that occurs with a single band. This is referred to as a Double-Band Bra. An X-Back increases support for the breasts by eliminating pressure on the neck from the halter. A Princess Seam instead of a dart in the Styling Cup enhances the contour.

The materials needed for these variations are listed below.

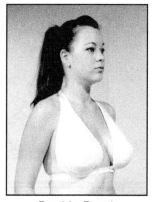
Double-Band

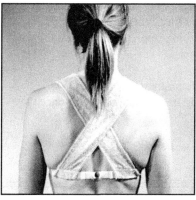
X-Back

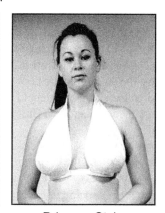
Princess Style

Qty	Items for Double-Band Bra
1 roll	Glad Press'n Seal
1 each	Masking Tape, 3/4" & 2" (2 & 5 cm)
1	Marking Pen
1	Posterboard 14" x 22" (36 x 56 cm)
1	Pattern paper 14 x 22" (36 x 56 cm)
1/2 yd	Muslin
1 yd	Elastic, 3/4" or 5/8" (20 or 16 mm)
1	G-Hook (optional)
6	Bra Strap Sliders (optional)

Qty	X-Back Bust Sling Bra
1 yd	Fashion Fabric
2 yds	3/8" (10 mm) Neckline Elastic
1 yd	3/4" (20 mm) Bra Band Elastic
1	3/4" (20 mm) Bra Strap Ring
2	3/4" (20 mm) Bra Strap Sliders
1	3/4" (20 mm) Bra Front Opening Clasp

The Double-Band Bust Sling Bra

A Double-Band Bust Sling Bra minimizes bust projection by giving the mold a more rounded appearance. The instructions that follow expand on the material for the Basic Bust Sling Bra which starts on page 63.

I. Create the Press'n Seal Mold

1. Use Press'n Seal to create the mold as described on page 65.
2. Apply masking tape to reinforce the shape created by the Press'n Seal. As you do this, refine the shape of the Bust Sling even further.
3. Add the basic design lines to the masking tape, including the outline of the Bust Sling where it meets the rib cage.
4. Remove the mold from the body.
5. Reinforce the inside of the mold with masking tape.
6. Separate the mold into two Bust Sling Bands that will be flat once they are cut.
7. Add sewing notches.
8. Cut the mold along the design lines.
9. Cut a dart in the Styling Cup.

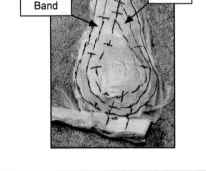

II. Create a Paper Pattern

1. To verifying the pattern shapes, transfer the mold to poster board.
2. Verify that the sewing notches line up.
3. Tape the poster board together to verify shaping.
4. Remove the tape from the posterboard.
5. Transfer the poster board shapes onto pattern paper.
6. Add 1/4" (6 mm) seam allowances.

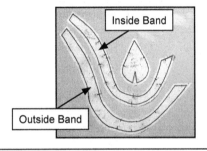

III. Create a Muslin Mock-Up

With the exceptions noted below, the procedure for sewing a Double-Band Bust Sling Bra is the same as for a single band.

1. Sew the Styling Cups' darts.
2. Pin the top of one Styling Cup to the inside of the inner Bust Sling Band.
3. Sew just a short length of the Styling Cup to the inside of the inner Bust Sling Band.
4. Pin the remainder of the Styling Cup to the inner Bust Sling Band.
5. Sew the inner Bust Sling Band to the Styling Cup.
6. Pin the top of the inner Bust Sling Band to the inside of the outer Bust Sling Band.
7. Sew a short length of the outer Bust Sling Band to the inner Bust Sling Band.
8. Pin the remainder of the outer Bust Sling Band to the inner Bust Sling Band.
9. Repeat steps 2 through 8 for the other Bust Sling Bands.
10. Finish the Bust Sling as described on page 71.

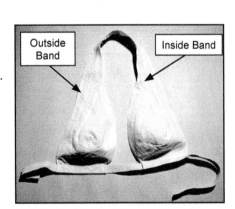

The X-Back Bust Sling Bra

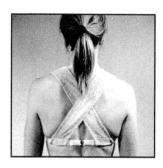

An X-Back Bust Sling Bra provides support for the front of a bra from the shoulder seam across the back down to the elastic at the rib cage.

The initial Bust Sling mold includes the shape required for the X-Back strap, see Step 10 on page 65. Use this shape to make a paper pattern.

Prepare an X-Back Muslin Mock-Up

1. Make a copy of the Bust Sling pattern less the halter portion of the neck.
2. Trace the end of the X-Bust Sling Band, then draw a rectangle that is 1-1/4" (3 cm) wide. This will be used as an elastic casing for the strap in back.
3. Cut the patterns out of muslin, then sew a trial muslin together as described on page 71.
4. Pin the elastic casing to the bottom of the strap, good sides together.
5. Sew a line of straight stitches using a 1/4" (6 mm) seam allowance.
6. Fold the elastic casing over the strap, wrong sides together, then sew along the top to create a 3/4" (20 mm) casing.
7. Thread elastic through the casing.
8. To verify fit, put the bra on.

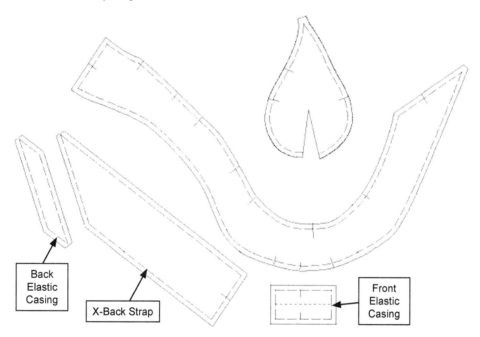

Back Elastic Casing

X-Back Strap

Front Elastic Casing

Pattern for an X-Back Bust Sling Bra

Sewing an X-Back Bust Sling Bra

These instructions show how to create an X-Back Bust Sling Bra out of non-stetch or powernet fabric.

1. Sew the Bust Sling Band.
2. Sew the Styling Cup.
3. Sew the Body of the Bust Sling.
4. Add the Rib Cage Elastic.

I. Sew the Bust Sling Band

1. Mark sewing notches on the fabric.
2. Sew the shoulder seam.
3. Press the shoulder seam open, then topstitch the seam allowances to the band using a 2 mm long, 2 mm wide zigzag stitch.
4. Trim off the excess seam allowance.
5. Pin the back elastic casing to the bottom of the X-Back strap, good sides together, then sew.
6. Use a zigzag stitch to sew the Bust Sling Band's seam allowance to the back elastic casing.
7. Trim off the excess seam allowance.
8. Repeat steps 2 through 7 for the other Bust Sling Band.

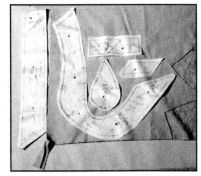

Cutting the X-Back Pattern

II. Sew the Styling Cup

1. Pin one of the Styling Cup's dart, then sew with a 1.5 mm straight stitch.
2. Use a triple overhand knot to tie off the threads across the dart point.
3. Press the dart allowance to the outside of the Styling Cup, then zigzag in place.
4. Pin the top of the Styling Cup to the inside of the Bust Sling Band, right sides together, then sew to the first sewing notch.
5. Pin the remainder of the Styling Cup to the Bust Sling Band, then sew.
6. Use a 2 mm zigzag to sew the Styling Cup's seam allowance to the Bust Sling Band, then trim off the excess seam allowance.
7. Repeat steps 1 through 6 for the other Bust Sling Band.

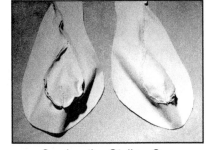

Sewing the Styling Cup

III. Sew the Body of the Bust Sling

1. To finish the front elastic casings' ends, turn the seam allowances to the inside then topstitch with a 2 mm zigzag stitch.
2. Turn one of the front elastic casings in half lengthwise, wrong side together, then pin it to the bottom of a Bust Sling Band.
3. Use a 2 mm zigzag to sew the neckline elastic around the entire Bust Sling Band. This neckline elastic should be sewn to the right side of the fashion fabric with the plush side up and the picot edge facing into the band.
4. Trim off the excess seam allowance.
5. Turn the neckline elastic to the inside of the Bust Sling Band, then sew with a 4 mm zigzag stitch.
6. Turn the back elastic casing's outside edges to the inside, then zigzag in place.
7. Pin the back elastic casing closed, then sew it with a straight stitch leaving the casing sufficiently open for the elastic to be pulled through.
8. Repeat steps 2 through 7 for the other Bust Sling Band.

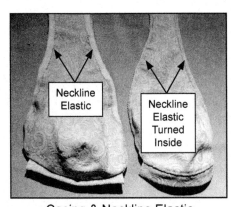

Neckline Elastic

Neckline Elastic Turned Inside

Casing & Neckline Elastic

IV. Add the Rib Cage Elastic
1. Cut two lengths of bra strap elastic for the rib cage.
2. Sew bra strap sliders to each end of the two lengths of elastic.
3. Thread the two elastics through a bra strap ring.
4. To thread the elastic through the casing, start at the back and continue until it emerges in the front.
5. Pin, then sew the front opening clasp to the rib cage elastic.

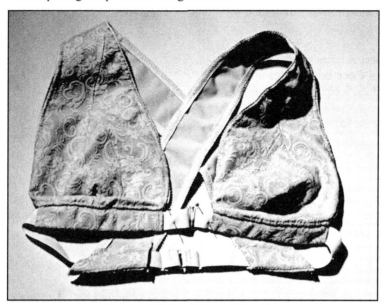

Finished X-Back Bust Sling Bra

Princess Seam Variations

A dart shapes fabric into a point. Depending on the fabric used and the size of the dart, this can be an appropriate shaping device. However, if shaping with a dart results in a rather abrupt point, changing it into a seam may be preferable. A seam commonly used in women's clothes is the Princess Seam, which is shaped from where a woman's arm breaks away from the body, then travels over the apex of the breast, continuing down to the rib cage.

The instructions in this section show how to create three variations of the Princess Seam:

- Princess Seam Styling Cup
- Two-Piece Princess Seam Bust Sling
- Three-Piece Princess Seam Bust Sling

These variations can be applied to any garment.

Princess Seam Styling Cup

1. Tape together a posterboard copy of the Bust Sling Styling Cup.
2. Use the posterboard to determine the shaping of the Princess Seam. A recommended location for the Princess Seam is close to where the arm breaks away from the body.
3. Draw the Princess Seam line on the posterboard.
4. Cut the Styling Cup, including the new Princess Seam.
5. Trace the cut sections onto a new sheet of posterboard.
6. Smooth the design lines and verify that the seam lines for both sides of the Princess Seam match.
7. Tape the Princess Seam Styling Cup together to verify its appearance and make any necessary adjustments.

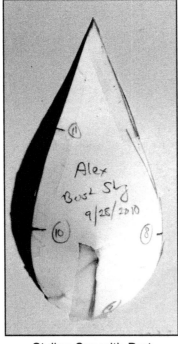
Styling Cup with Dart

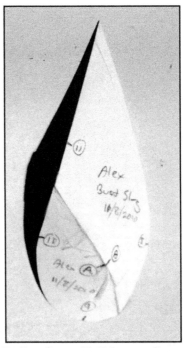
Styling Cup with Princess Seam

Two-Piece Princess Seam Bust Sling

The Princess Seam can be extended to include the entire lower portion of the Bust Sling.

1. Tape together a posterboard copy of the Bust Sling Band and Styling Cup.
2. Use the posterboard to determine the shaping of the Princess Seam.
3. Draw the Princess Seam line on the posterboard.
4. Cut the Bust Sling, including the new Princess Seam.
5. Trace the cut sections onto a new sheet of posterboard.
6. Smooth the design lines and verify that the seam lines for both sides of the Princess Seam match.
7. Tape the Princess Seam together to verify its appearance and make any necessary adjustments.

Two-Piece Pattern   Two-Piece Taped

Three-Piece Princess Seam Bust Sling

For a more gradual contour, add an additional seam to the lower portion of the two-piece Princess Seam.

1. Tape together a posterboard copy of the Bust Sling Band and Styling Cup.
2. Use the posterboard to determine the shaping of the Princess Seam.
3. Draw the Princess Seam line on the posterboard.
4. Cut the Bust Sling, including the new Princess Seam.
5. Trace the cut sections onto a new sheet of posterboard.
6. Smooth the design lines and verify that the seam lines for both sides of the Princess Seam match.
7. Tape the Princess Seam together to verify its appearance and make any necessary adjustments.

 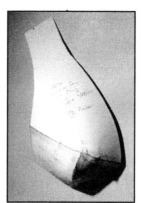

Three-Piece Pattern   Three-Piece Taped

Bust Sling Bra Designs

The basic Bust Sling pattern can be styled into a variety of bras. The techniques for creating the different bras can be interchanged.

The Hybrid Bust Sling Bra combines the basic Bust Sling Bra with the rib cage portion of a conventional bra. This helps secure the location of the Bust Slings and controls any fluff on the side of the body. The Racerback Bust Sling provides additional support across the back. A zipper front is convenient for people with mobility issues. And the Nursing Bra has obvious applications.

The materials you will need for these bras are listed below. The degree of stretch in a specific elastic can vary. For each of these styles, adjust the length of the rib cage elastic for the wearer's comfort.

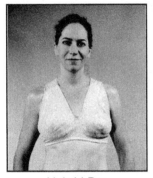 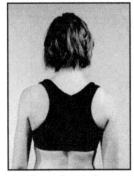 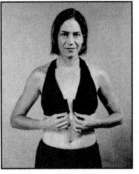 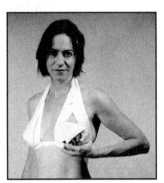

| Hybrid Bra | Racerback Bra | Zipper Front Bra | Nursing Bra |

Qty	Hybrid Bust Sling Bra
1/2 yd	Fashion Fabric
2 yds	3/8" Bra Band Elastic
1 yd	3/4" Bra Band Elastic
1	Bra Back Hook & Eye Tape

Qty	Racerback Bust Sling Bra
1/2 yd	Muslin
1/2 yd	Pattern Paper
1/2 yd	Fashion Fabric
2 yds	1/4" Elastic
1 yd	3/4" Elastic
1	Bra Front Opening Clasp

Qty	Zipper Front Bust Sling Bra
1/2 yd	Fashion Fabric
2 yds	Neckline Elastic
6"	Zipper
1 yd	3/4" Bra Strap Elastic
3	3/4" Bra Strap Sliders

Qty	Hybrid Bust Sling Bra
1/2 yd	Fashion Fabric
2 yds	Fold-Over Elastic
1 yd	3/4" Bra Strap Elastic
1	3/4" Bra Strap SLider
1	3/4" G-Hook
2	Waistband Hook & Eye

Rib Cage Expansion for Breathing

The circumference of the rib cage changes when a person breathes. This can be seen by measuring the rib cage twice: when the wearer inhales fully; then exhales.

The Bust Sling Bra design requires a good fit at the rib cage. The length of the elastic at the rib cage should be adjusted for the specific material used and the wearer's comfort. For some designs, eliminating the elastic may be possible–in which case, the fit at the rib cage should be from the inhale measurement.

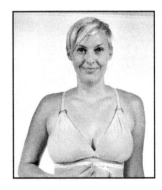

Inhale	Exhale	Elastic

Hybrid Bust Sling Bra

The Hybrid Bra combines the Bust Sling's support of the breasts with the Rib Cage Band of a conventional bra. The Rib Cage Band optimizes the position of the Bust Sling in front and provides support for soft tissue fluff on the side of the body. The Bust Sling eliminates the need for an underwire.

This example uses the bra findings of a conventional bra, including plush back elastic at the rib cage, plush back elastic or neckline edging around the Bust Sling Band, and a hook & eye bra back closing. This style does not require bra strap elastic, sliders, underwires, or underwire channeling.

This Hybrid Bra requires the full band pattern of a conventional bra which includes a bridge and back band as shown below. In this illustration, there is a dotted line at the vertical Bust Apex line and Center Front. The fabric for the band can be powernet by itself, or powernet with a fashion fabric cover.

Prepare the Pattern for a Hybrid Bust Sling Bra

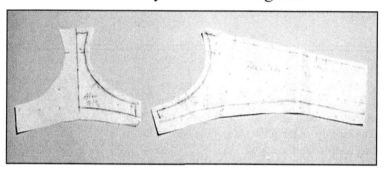

The Rib Cage Band Pattern

The Hybrid Bra uses a conventional bra's band and bridge patterns, see page 119 for details. Alternatively, cut out the cups from a conventional bra that is no longer wearable, then trace the band's outline.

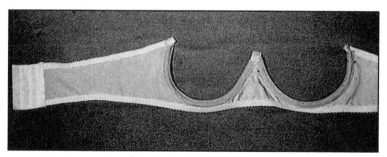

Bra Band without Cups

Sewing the Hybrid Bra

The Hybrid Bust Sling Bra can be made with either a halter neck or X-Back. These instructions use the X-Back described on page 75.

I. Sew the Back Band to the Bust Sling

1. Pin the lining to the fashion fabric for the bridge, wrong sides together, then zigzag around the edge with a 4 mm zigzag.
2. Pin the back band to the bridge at the Apex seam, right sides together, then sew.
3. Press open the seam. Topstitch it with a 2 mm zigzag, then trim off the excess.
4. Pin the Bust Sling to the back band, matching the apex seam to the apex sewing notch on the Bust Sling Band, right sides together, then sew with a 2 mm straight stitch.
5. Press, topstitch the seam allowance with a 2 mm zigzag, then trim.

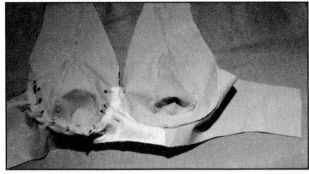

Sewing the Hybrid Bra Body

II. Add the Bra Band Elastic

1. Sew 3/4" (2 cm) plush back elastic to the bottom of the bra, aligning the elastic's edge to the bottom of the back band and bridge. Use a 2 mm zigzag stitch along the elastic's top edge. The plush back should be face up on the good side of the band with the picot edge facing away from the edge.
2. Trim off the excess seam allowance, then turn the elastic to the inside and hand baste in place. As you baste, align the picot edge so it just shows along the bottom of the bra.
3. Using a 4 mm or triple-step zigzag, topstitch the elastic along the top edge, then remove the basting.
4. Sew 3/8" (9 mm) plush back elastic to the edges of the bra, aligning the edge of the elastic to the edge of the bra. Use a 2 mm zigzag stitch along the inside edge of the elastic. The plush back should be face up on the good side of the band with the picot edge facing away from the edge.
5. Trim off the excess seam allowance, then turn the elastic to the inside and hand baste in place. As you baste, align the picot edge so it just shows along the edge of the bra.
6. Using a 4 mm or triple-step zigzag, topstitch the elastic along the edge.

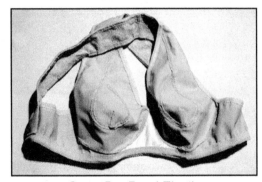

Sewn Bra Band Elastic

III. Finish the Bra

Complete the bra by attaching the X-Back to the rib cage, then adding hook-and-eye tape.

To sew hook-and-eye tape, sandwich the back band between the tape's fashion fabric side and the plush side as illustrated below.

1. Using a 2 mm straight stitch, sew the eye closure's inside to the wrong side of the left back band.

2. Fold the eye closure's fashion side over the good side of the back band, then sew in place.

3. Sew the hook closure's fashion side to the good side of the back band.

4. Fold the hook closure's inside to the wrong side of the back band, then sew in place.

5. Verify the position of the "X" band in a fitting, then sew in place.

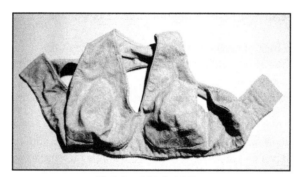

Finished Hybrid Bra

Racerback Bust Sling Bra

       The Racerback style provides support across a wide portion of the back. The pattern can be created by either draping fabric across the back or by using a Bodice Sloper pattern for the back.

       When working with a partner or making a bra for another person, draw the design lines for the Racerback, as described in Steps 7 & 8 below. Using gingham will make it easier to verify the grain of the fabric is correctly positioned.

       When creating the Racerback as a do-it-yourself (DIY) process, it will be easier to draw the design lines after the fabric is removed from the body. Muslin works fine for this process.

I. Draping the Racerback Pattern

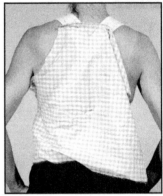

1. Prepare a piece of gingham with a line in the center for Center Back.
2. Put a safety pin at the top and bottom of the Center Back line for guidance.
3. Put on a Bust Sling Bra muslin mock-up.
4. Tape the gingham back at the shoulders verifying that the Center Back is aligned with the spine.
5. Tape the gingham to one side of the bust sling, then verify that the Center Back has not been pulled out of alignment.
6. Secure the gingham to the Bust Sling with pins at the shoulder and the side.
7. Mark where the shoulder seam of the Bust Sling front intersects with the gingham back.
8. Mark where the side of the Bust Sling Band intersects with the side of the gingham for the top of the racerback. Indicate the top of the rib cage elastic.
9. Remove the Bust Sling mock-up and gingham.

Draping a Racerback

II. Adjust the Muslin Drape

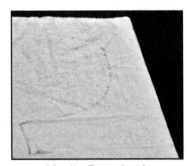

If you are working with a partner or making a bra for another person, you can add the design lines while the fabric is draped on the body. If you are creating a racerback as a do-it-yourself process, the design lines can be refined after you have removed the fabric. For this example, muslin is used.

1. Mark the location of the shoulder seam from the Bust Sling Bra on the muslin for the Racerback.
2. Mark the location where the Racerback coincides with the side of the Bust Sling at the rib cage level.
3. Remove the muslin from the Bust Sling.
4. Fold the muslin at Center Back.
5. Draw in the bottom of the Racerback at right angles to the Center Back. This is the top of the rib cage elastic.
6. Draw the arm side of the Racerback from the outside of the shoulder seam down to the side of the Bust Sling Band.
7. Draw in the desired back neckline.

Muslin Racerback

III. Create a Paper Pattern for the Racerback

1. Place a piece of pattern paper on top of the muslin.
2. Trace the rib cage, Center Back, shoulder seam, arm opening, and side seam lines.
3. Draw in a line at the bottom of the pattern to indicate the width of the rib cage elastic.
4. Add an elastic allowance to the bottom of the pattern established in Step 3.
5. Add a 1/4" (6 mm) seam allowance around the arm and the neckline.
6. Add a seam allowance at the side seam and shoulder seam. I recommend starting with a 1" (25 mm) seam allowance to verify the fit.
7. When you use a V shape for the back neckline, create a pattern by tracing the back V shape. This will be the back facing.

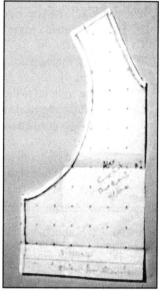

Racerback Pattern

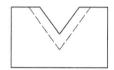

Back Facing

IV. Front Patterns

The side of the Bust Sling's Band and elastic casing needs to be extended to connect to the Racerback. This can be determined while you are draping the back pattern.

1. Create a copy of the elastic casing pattern.
2. Extend the elastic casing pattern to the side by the same amount the Bust Sling has been extended.
3. For a front opening closure device, extend the elastic casing pattern's Center Front side by adding 1-1/2" (38 mm) to the front edge.
4. Add a 1/4" (6 mm) seam allowance to the top of the front elastic band and a 1" (25 mm) seam allowance to the side.
5. Cut the Racerback from the fashion fabric.
6. Sew the two Bust Slings for the front.

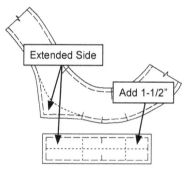

Extended Side

Add 1-1/2"

V. Sew the Racerback to the Bust Sling

1. Pin the Bust Sling front's shoulder seam to the Racerback, then sew.
2. Use a zigzag stitch to sew 1/4" (6 mm) elastic to the side of the Bust Sling Band and Racerback. Sew the elastic to the wrong side of the fashion fabric.
3. Turn the elastic to the inside and topstitch in place with a 4 mm zigzag stitch.
4. Pin the elastic casing to the bottom of the Bust Sling, right sides together, then sew.

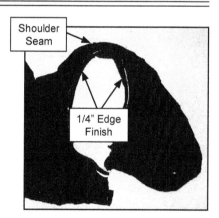

Shoulder Seam

1/4" Edge Finish

VI. Sew the Back of the Racerback

1. Turn the outside edges of the V reinforcement facing and topstitch with a zigzag stitch.
2. Pin the V facing piece to the fashion fabric, right sides together, then sew with a straight stitch. Sew 1/4" (6 mm) elastic to the wrong side of the Bust Sling from the front up to the back V.
3. Trim off the elastic, leaving some excess elastic below the V.
4. Sew 1/4" (6 mm) elastic to the other side of the neckline.
5. Trim off the elastic, leaving some excess elastic below the V.
6. Use a seam ripper to trim the V right to the stitching.
7. Turn the neckline elastic to the inside, then topstitch with a zigzag.
8. Trim off the excess elastic at the bottom of the V shape.

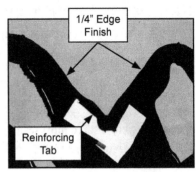

VI. Finish the Racerback Bust Sling Bra

1. Pin the side seam along the rib cage elastic tab, right side together, then sew. Until you have verified the fit, I recommend you do not sew the Bust Sling to the Racerback any higher than the elastic.
2. Sew 3/4" (2 cm) elastic on the wrong side of the bottom of the Bust Sling Racerback. I recommend using zigzag stitches along both the top and bottom of the elastic. Keep most of the stretch around the back.
3. Roll the elastic to the inside, then sew along the top of the elastic to secure it in place.
4. Verify the fit. Adjust the side seam as necessary.
5. Sew the front closing device in place.

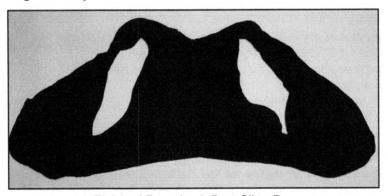

Finished Racerback Bust Sling Bra

Zipper-Front Bust Sling Bra

These instructions illustrate how to add a bridge to the Center Front. To create the bridge pattern, use muslin to determine the shape as described for the second fitting on page 71. If you have a bridge pattern for a conventional bra, use that. The top of the bridge should at least reach the level of the Apex. The space between the breasts needs to be at least 1" to accommodate a zipper.

In this example, a zipper is used with the bridge to create a front opening, halter style bra.

I. Prepare the Bridge

1. The bottom of the bridge pattern must include the Bust Sling's elastic casing.
2. Measuring from Center Front, shorten the Bust Sling Band elastic casing by the width of the bridge.
3. For a zipper opening, add a 1/2" (12 mm) seam allowance to Center Front.
4. Cut the bridge from both fashion fabric and lining.
5. Pin the top and bottom of the bridge lining to the fashion fabric, right sides together, then sew with a 2 mm straight stitch.
6. Turn the bridge right side out, then use a 4 mm zigzag to sew the unfinished edges.
7. Pin the Center Front seam of the bridge, then baste with a 5 mm straight stitch.
8. Press the Center Front seam open, then use a zipper foot to sew the zipper to the inside of the bridge, aligning the bottom of the separating zipper with the bottom of the bridge.
9. Remove the basting, then lower the zipper pull.
10. To prevent the zipper pull from coming off the top of the zipper, sew across its top.

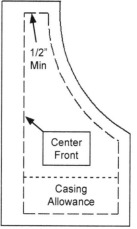

1/2"
Min

Center
Front

Casing
Allowance

Bridge Pattern

II. Finish the Bra

1. Pin, then sew the elastic casing to the sides of the bridge.
2. Press the seam allowances toward Center Front, then zigzag in place.
3. Pin the elastic casing and bridge to the Bust Sling Band, then sew with a 2 mm straight stitch.
4. Sew the neckline edging to the edge of the Bust Sling.
5. Trim the seam allowance, then turn the elastic under and zigzag in place.
6. To allow adjustment of the rib cage elastic for tension, add bra strap sliders at Center Back.
7. Slide the rib cage elastic into the elastic casing, then zigzag the end.

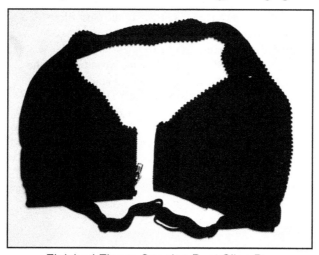

Finished Zipper-Opening Bust Sling Bra

Bust Sling Nursing Bra

The open cup Bust Sling Band is a natural shape for a Nursing Bra. The only addition that needs to be made is an expanded Nursing Cup to cover the opening. In this example, the princess seam Styling Cup is used, see page 78. And the top of the Nursing Cup is fastened to the Bust Sling Band using a wide waistband hook & eye.

I. Create the Styling Cup Pattern

1. Tape together a poster board copy of the basic Bust Sling Bra.
2. On the Bust Sling Band, add 1" (25 mm) to expand around the edges of the Styling Cup.
3. Create a 1" (25 mm) tab at the top of the expanded Styling Cup.
4. Cut the poster board along the lines added in Step 2 & 3. This becomes the shape for the Nursing Cup.
5. Cut along the line of the Princess Seam.
6. Add a second seam line to the bottom of the Nursing Cup. This creates a three-piece Nursing Cup.
7. Trace the shapes onto pattern paper.
8. Add 1/4" (6 mm) seam allowance to all edges except the top.
9. Add a 1/2" (12 mm) seam allowance to the top of the Nursing Cup.

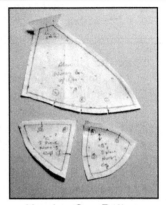

Nursing Cup Pattern

II. Sew the Inside Band

1. Use the patterns to cut out the fashion fabric.
2. Remove the pattern from the Bust Sling Band and pin the vertical seam that joins the inside and outside. Verify that you have a left and right Bust Sling Band.
3. Sew from the top of the vertical seam to 1/4" (6 mm) from the bottom of the vertical seam. This 1/4" (6 mm) allows the seam allowance to be turned under at the top of the open cup area.
4. Stay stitch 1/4" (6 mm) around the inside of the open cup area, then turn under the seam allowance.
5. Use a 2 mm zigzag to topstitch the open cup seam allowance in place, then trim off the excess.

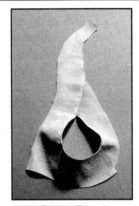

Sewn Band

III. Finish the Bust Sling Band

1. Sew the elastic casing, then pin to the bottom of the Bust Sling Band.
2. Topstitch the elastic casing's seam allowance to the body of the Bust Sling Band with a 2 mm zigzag stitch, then trim the seam allowance.
3. For a halter style, sew the Center Back seam.
4. Starting from the outer edge of the Bust Sling Band, sew the wrong side of the fold-over elastic to the wrong side of the Bust Sling Band. As you sew, align the edge of the band with the center of the fold-over elastic.
5. Turn the fold-over elastic to the right side of the band, then zigzag in place.

Fold-Over Edging

IV. Sew the Styling Cup

1. Pin, then sew the Styling Cup along the Princess Seam.
2. Press open the seam, zigzag the seam allowances flat, then trim.
3. Pin the bottom of the Nursing Cup to the top, right sides together, then sew.
4. Press open the seam, zigzag the seam allowances flat, then trim.
5. Zigzag the top of the Nursing Cup, then fold it over and press to the inside.
6. Stay stitch 1/4" (6 mm) around the edge of the Nursing Cup, then turn under the seam allowance.
7. Use a 2 mm zigzag to topstitch the edge of the Nursing Cup in place, then trim off the excess.

Inside of Styling Cup   Outside of Styling Cup

V. Finish the Bust Sling Nursing Bra

1. Pin the Nursing Cup to the bottom of the open-cup Bust Sling Band, then machine baste in place.
2. Sew a waistband hook & eye to attach the top of the Nursing Cup to the Bust Sling Band.
3. Sew a G-Hook to the rib cage elastic.
4. Thread the elastic through the elastic casing at the bottom of the Bust Sling.
5. Sew a loop at the other end of the rib cage elastic.

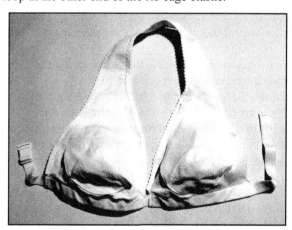

Finished Bust Sling Nursing Bra

Bust Sling Garment Designs

The basic Bust Sling pattern can be styled into a variety of garments including swimsuit tops, empire style dresses, gowns, compression tops, and wedding dresses.

For garments extended below the rib cage, use a simple skirt pattern. The skirt can be added to the Bust Sling Top with a non-stretch Rib Cage Band and zipper or by finishing the skirt's top edge with plush elastic.

For the wedding dress designs see page 148.

The materials necessary for the garments in this chapter are listed below.

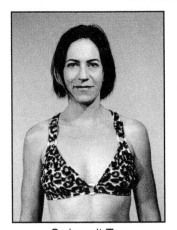

Swimsuit Top

Dress

Gown

Dream Shaper

Qty	Swimsuit Top
1/2 yd	Fashion Fabric
1/2 yd	Lining Fabric
5	Swimsuit Rings
1 yd	1/4" Elastic
1 yd	3/4" Elastic

Qty	Skirt Pattern
2 yds	Muslin
2 yds	Pattern Paper

Qty	Dress & Gown
1/2 yd	Fashion Fabric
2 yds	1/4" Elastic
1 yd	3/4" Elastic
1	Hook & Eye

Qty	Dream Shaper
1 yd	Compression Lycra
2 yds	1/4" Elastic
1yd	3/4" Plush Elastic
2	Bra Cups

Draping a Skirt

The process for draping this skirt pattern is the same as described for the Bikini Top, see page 27.

1. Prepare two rectangles of muslin that are more than half the circumference of the hips and long enough to reach mid thigh.
2. Fold the two pieces of muslin in half lengthwise and mark vertical lines at the fold. These are the Center Front and Center Back lines.
3. Pin the top of the Center Front line to the Bust Sling Mock Up at the rib cage.
4. Adjust the muslin skirt to lay smoothly over the body while keeping the Center Front vertical, then pin as necessary along the rib cage.
5. Pin the top of the Center Back line to the Bust Sling Mock Up at the rib cage.
6. Adjust the muslin skirt to lay smoothly over the body while keeping the Center Back vertical and pin as necessary along the rib cage.
7. To hold the back muslin in place, pin it to the rib cage.
8. Mark the waistline for half the body from Center Front to Center Back along the Rib Cage Band of the Bust Sling Mock Up.
9. Pin or tape the side seam so it hangs straight down the body.
10. Create paper patterns from the fitted shapes.
11. Add 1" (2.5 cm) seam allowance to the side seams and 3/4" (2 cm) seam allowance to the waist seam.

The Rib Cage Band Pattern

A Rib Cage Band should be long enough that the wearer can breathe comfortably, see page 80. It usually has a Center Back opening.

1. Draw a horizontal line that is the length of the Rib Cage measurement, see page 80.
2. Draw vertical lines on both ends of this line, then mark the Rib Cage Band's desired height. This is commonly 1" (2.5 cm) to 1-1/2" (4 cm).
3. For the Center Front, draw a vertical line half way between the ends.
4. To add a hook-and-eye closure, extend the right end of the pattern by 1-1/2" (4 cm).
5. For seam allowances that match the other pattern pieces, add 1/4" (6 mm) to the top, 3/4" (4 cm) to the bottom, and 1" (2.5 cm) to the ends.

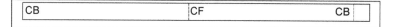

Sewing the Bust Sling Top for a Garment

A Bust Sling Top for garments can be finished with elastic, like a Bust Sling Bra, or have a separate Rib Cage Band. To sew a Halter Neck, see page 92.

1. Use the Bust Sling patterns to cut both the fashion fabric and the lining.
2. Use the fashion fabric to sew the Bust Sling Top.
3. Use the same sequence to sew the lining fabric.
4. Pin the fashion fabric to the lining, right sides together, then sew along the inside and outside edges of the Bust Sling.
5. Turn the Bust Sling right side out.
6. Zigzag the bottom edge of the Bust Sling fashion fabric to the lining.

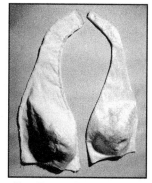

Top Sewn then Turned

Sewing a Garment with a Rib Cage Band

A Rib Cage Band can be used with or without elastic. When the Rib Cage Band and skirt are made from non-stretch fabric, use a Center Back seam for the skirt and add a zipper.

1. Use the skirt patterns to cut the fashion fabric.
2. Use the Rib Cage Band pattern to cut both the fashion fabric and the lining material.
3. When working with woven fabric, prevent fraying by zigzagging the edges.
4. Sew the skirt's two back panels together along the Center Back seam, right sides together. The top of this seam should be a basting stitch 12" (30 cm) long.
5. Hand baste the zipper to the top of the Center Back seam.
6. Use a zipper foot to sew the zipper to the Center Back seam.
7. To test the zipper, remove the basting, then open the zipper.
8. Pin the skirt's front and back side seams together, then sew and press open.
9. Pin the Rib Cage Band's fashion fabric to the top of the skirt, right sides together, then sew.
10. Pin the Bust Sling Top to the Rib Cage Band, right sides together, then sew.
11. Pin the Rib Cage Band's lining to the fashion fabric with the Bust Sling sandwiched between the two layers, then sew.
12. Pin the bottom of the Rib Cage Band's lining to the seam from Step 7 and hand stitch in place.
13. Add a hook & eye at Center Back.

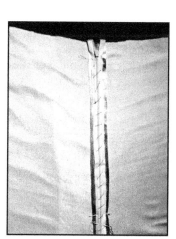

Hand Basted Zipper

Sewing a Garment with Plush Elastic

Several garments are described that use knit material. The top of the skirt for these garments can be finished with plush elastic. Several factors need to be considered.

- Verify that both the elastic and the knit skirt fabric can be stretched enough for the garment to be pulled on over the head or the hips.
- Establish the length for the plush elastic to the wearer's specification for snugness and comfort.
- Adjust the skirt's waist seam allowance to the width of the plush elastic being used. This becomes an elastic allowance.
- When plush elastic's decorative edge is positioned on the edge of the skirt, it will not be visible in the finished garment.
- When the decorative edge faces the body of the skirt, the decorative edge will be visible as described on page 18.

Pull Over Measurement

_____

1. Use the skirt patterns to cut the fashion fabric. The direction of maximum stretch should be around the body.
2. Pin the skirt's front and back side seams together, then sew and press open.
3. Pin the Bust Sling Tops to the skirt at Center Front, right sides together, then sew.
4. Cut a length of plush elastic to the rib cage measurement plus 1" (2.5 cm).

5. Pin the plush elastic in a loop with a 1" (2.5 cm) overlap, then sew closed with a 2 mm zigzag stitch.
6. Pin the plush elastic to the fashion fabric with the Bust Sling sandwiched between the two layers.
7. Use a 2 mm zigzag stitch to sew the elastic to the skirt. The stitching should be on the edge closest to the body of the skirt.
8. Trim off the excess elastic allowance.
9. Turn the elastic to the inside of the skirt and zigzag in place.

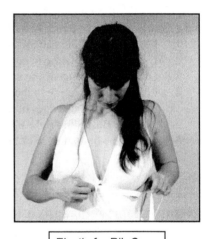

Elastic for Rib Cage

_____

Sewing Tip for Lined Halter Tops

When a halter neck is lined and has a Center Back seam, it is easy to turn the Bust Sling Top right side out.

1. On one side of the Bust Sling Top pin back the lining by the amount of the seam allowance, then sew the fashion fabric to the lining. This creates a tube-like opening at Center Back.
2. Sew the other side of the Bust Sling Top.
3. Pin the two Bust Sling Tops on the Center Back seam, right sides together.
4. Sew the Center Back seam without catching the lining from Step 1.
5. Push the Center Back seam allowances through the tube created in Step 1.
6. To finish the lining, hand stitch the two sides of the lining together.

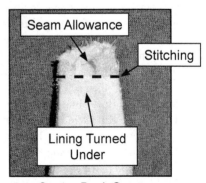

Seam Allowance

Stitching

Lining Turned Under

Center Back Seam

A Bust Sling Swimsuit Top

This Swimsuit Top, made from cotton Lycra with a cotton T-Shirt knit for an underlining, has a two-piece princess seam. It has rings located at the top, Center Front, and sides. The rings along the bottom are secured using 3/4" (2 cm) swimsuit elastic. The straps are made from fashion fabric using 1" (25 mm) elastic and then secured with buckles.

To create the pattern for the Swimsuit Top, start by taping together a poster board copy of the two-piece princess seam pattern.

I. Create the Bottom Half of the Swimsuit Top

1. Draw the Apex center line up to the top of the Bust Sling pattern.
2. Draw in the design lines of the Swimsuit Top.
3. Cut apart the poster board.
4. Trace the bottom part of the princess pattern, then mark the sewing notches.
5. At the bottom of the pattern, add the width of the 3/4" (2 cm) rib cage elastic. This will be the finished edge of the Swimsuit Top.
6. For the elastic allowance, draw a second line down to the finished edge of the pattern.
7. For the ring overlap, extend the lines for the elastic out 1" (25 mm) from the outside of the pattern.
8. Add 1/4" (6 mm) seam allowances to the remainder of the pattern.

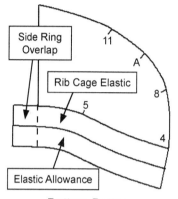

Bottom Pattern

II. Create the Top Half of the Swimsuit Top

1. Trace the top of the Swimsuit Top pattern, including the Apex Center Line.
2. Add a 1" (25 mm) flap to the top of the pattern for securing the ring.
3. Match the two pattern pieces at the bottom of the princess seam, then extend the lines for the elastic onto the top piece.
4. Extend the lines for the elastic out 1" (25 mm) from the front of the pattern for the Center Front, CF, ring overlap.
5. Add 1/4" (6 mm) seam allowances to the remaining seam lines.
6. To attain the correct shape for the overlap, fold under the top-ring overlap before cutting out the pattern.

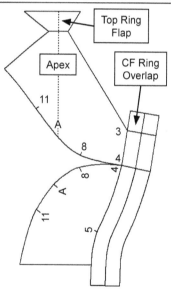

Elastic Allowance
Added to Princess Top

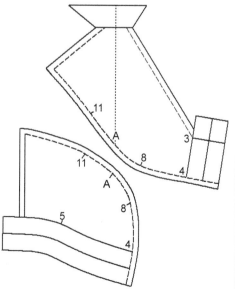

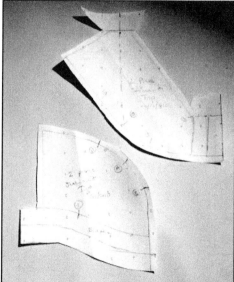

Completed Swimsuit Top Pattern

III. Sew the Body of the Swimsuit Top

  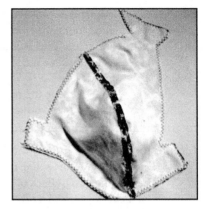

1. Use the patterns to cut the fashion fabric and lining.
2. Using a 4 mm zigzag stitch, sew the lining fabric to the fashion fabric, then press.
3. Transfer the sewing notches for the princess seam to the fabric.

4. Pin the fabric along the princess seam, right sides together, then sew with a 1 mm zigzag or stretch stitch.

5. To topstitch the seam allowance in place, press open and use a 2 mm zigzag stitch, then trim off the excess seam allowance.

IV. Sew the Elastic

 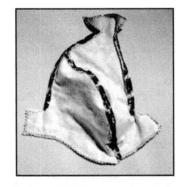 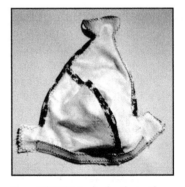

1. Using a 3 mm zigzag stitch, sew 1/4" (6 mm) elastic to the Swimsuit Top's wrong side along the inside and outside edges.

2. To topstitch the elastic in place, turn the elastic to the inside of the Swimsuit Top, then sew a 3 mm zigzag.

3. Sew 3/4" (2 cm) elastic to the Swimsuit Top's wrong side, aligning it to the lower edge.

4. Turn the elastic to the inside, then topstitch it along the top edge of the elastic.

V. Sew the Rings

1. Thread a ring through the Swimsuit Top's tab, then pin the overlap in place.
2. Using a zipper foot, sew the ring in place with a straight stitch.

3. Change to a regular foot and topstitch with a 2 mm zigzag stitch, then trim off the excess overlap.

4. Thread a ring through the elastic on the outside of the Swimsuit Top, then pin the overlap in place.
5. Using a zipper foot, sew the ring in place with a straight stitch.
6. Change to a regular foot and topstitch with a 2 mm zigzag stitch, then trim off the excess elastic overlap for each of the rings.

V. Fashion Fabric Straps

In this example, straps are created with a buckle for securing them to the Swimsuit Top like bra strap sliders, thereby allowing for different strapping configurations such as the X-Back and Halter Top shown in the pictures below.

1. Cut the fashion fabric to the strap length desired and at least 3 times the width of the elastic.
2. Using a 4 mm zigzag, sew one edge of the fashion fabric to one edge of the elastic.
3. Wrap the fashion fabric around the elastic, then topstitch down the center of the strap. Use either a regular zigzag or triple-step zigzag stitch.
4. Trim off the excess fabric.
5. Sew a buckle to one end of the strap.

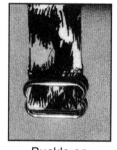

Buckle on
Fashion Fabric
Strap

 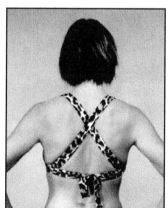 

Buckled Straps   X-Back Straps   Halter Neck Straps

Bust Sling Dress

This dress uses the three-piece princess seam pattern and X-Back straps. There is a zipper closing with hook and eye at Center Back. The skirt is attached to a 1" (25 mm) band around the rib cage. The Rib Cage Band is reinforced using fusible interfacing and has side seams to allow for fitting adjustments.

Note: Whenever you are working with a new version of a pattern, you should sew an initial trial version, basting any seams that may require additional fittings.

I. Sew for a Trial Fitting

1. Using the patterns, cut the fabric.
2. To prevent fraying, zigzag the edges of the skirt and Rib Cage Band.
3. Sew a zipper at Center Back, see page 91.
4. Interface the fashion fabric Rib Cage Band with fusible interfacing.
5. Sew the Rib Cage Bands to the top of the skirt.
6. Sew the side seams, then press.
7. Using the fashion fabric, pin the two sides of the princess seam's lower portion, right sides together, then sew.
8. Press the seam allowance open, then topstitch in place with a 2 mm zigzag and trim.
9. Pin the top of the princess seam to the bottom, right sides together, then sew.
10. Press the seam allowance open, then topstitch in place with a 2 mm zigzag and trim.
11. Pin the X-Back strap to the top of the front, then sew.
12. Use the same sequence to sew the lining fabric.
13. Pin the fashion fabric to the lining, right sides together, then sew along the Bust Sling's inside and outside edges.
14. Turn the Bust Sling right side out.
15. Zigzag the bottom edge of the Bust Sling fashion fabric to the lining.
16. Pin the Bust Sling to the Rib Cage Band, right sides together, then machine baste.

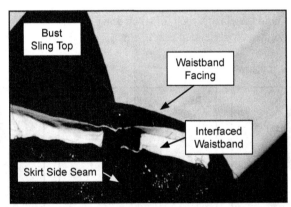

II. Finishing the Dress

1. Edge stitch along the Bust Sling's outside and inside.
2. Pin a facing to the Rib Cage Band, then sew along the ends and top edge.
3. Turn the facing to the inside, then pin under the bottom seam allowance.
4. Sew the bottom of the rib cage facing.
5. Sew a hook and a loop to the ends of the Rib Cage Band.

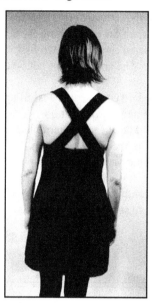

The Finished Dress

Bust Sling Gown

This full length gown has a top that is made from 6 vertical bands and an X-Back.
It uses a zipper closing at the skirt's Center Back as well as a Rib Cage Band with a tab
overlap and waistband hook & eye.

I. Create the Pattern

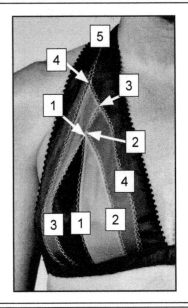

The Bust Sling panels are not that obvious, so a trial top of contrasting fabric
illustrates the seams. This is important for establishing the sewing sequence. Any
seam that dead ends into another seam should be sewn first. The numbers indicate
the sewing sequence for the seams. The arrows point out where the seams dead
end.

1. Tape together a poster board copy of the Bust Sling Bra.
2. Draw in the lines for the new seam locations.
3. Mark sewing notches and label each pattern clearly.
4. Cut the poster board along the new seam lines.
5. Trace the poster board onto pattern paper.
6. Add 1/4" (6 mm) seam allowances to all seams.
7. Cut the patterns out in contrasting colors of scrap fabric.
8. Determine the appropriate sewing sequence, then sew the panels
   together.

II. Sew the Bust Sling Top

1. Use the Bust Sling Top patterns to cut the fashion fabric and the lining.
2. Mark the sewing notches and label the pattern pieces.
3. Pin the lining fabric according to the sewing sequence shown above,
   then sew each of the panels.
4. Press open the seams, then sew the seam allowances flat using a 2 mm
   zigzag stitch.
5. Clip off the excess seam allowances.
6. Pin the X-Back strap to the Bust Sling front, then sew.
7. Following the same sequence, sew the Bust Sling Top in the fashion
   fabric.
8. Pin the lining to the fashion fabric, right sides together, along the inside
   and outside edges, then sew.
9. Press open the seam allowances, then turn the Bust Sling Top's right
   sides out.
10. Edge stitch the top.
11. Pin the bottom of the Bust Sling Top, then zigzag the fashion fabric to
    the lining along the bottom edge.

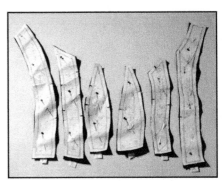

Patterns for the Bust Sling Top

III. Sew the Skirt

The gown's skirt is sewn using standard sewing techniques. The appropriate steps are listed below. This example, made from sheer fabric, includes a lining for the skirt that stops above the knee.

1. Using the skirt patterns from page 90, cut the fashion fabric for the full length gown.
2. Zigzag the skirt's edges to prevent fraying.
3. Sew a zipper at Center Back.
4. Pin the side seams, good sides together, then sew.
5. Use a rolled hem to finish the bottom of the skirt.
6. Use the skirt patterns to cut the lining.
7. Zigzag the lining's edges to prevent fraying.
8. Pin the Center Back seam, right sides together, leaving the top open to accommodate the zipper, then sew.
9. Pin the side seams, good sides together, then sew.
10. Use a rolled hem to finish the bottom of the lining.
11. Along the waist, pin the lining inside the fashion fabric, wrong sides together.
12. Use a zigzag stitch to sew the lining to the fashion fabric along the edge of the waist's seam allowance.
13. Hand stitch the lining around the zipper.

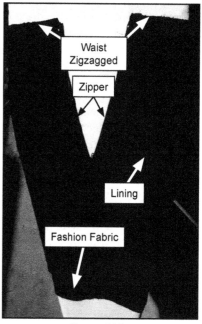

Sewn Skirt

IV. Finish the Gown

To finish the gown, sew the Bust Sling top to the Rib Cage Band, then sew the skirt to the other side of the Rib Cage Band.

1. Pin the Rib Cage Band at the side seams, then sew.
2. Pin the Bust Sling Top between the Rib Cage Band's fashion fabric and lining, then sew.
3. Pin the skirt to the fashion fabric Rib Cage Band, right sides together, then sew.
4. Pin the bottom of the rib cage lining to the inside of the skirt and hand finish.
5. Hand sew the X-Back straps to the Rib Cage Band.
6. Sew a hook and eye to the Center Back overlap.

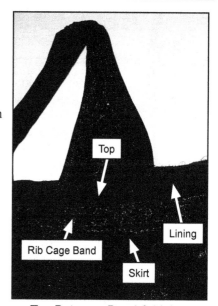

Top Between Band & Lining

The Finished Gown

Bust Sling Dream Shaper

The Dream Shaper uses compression fabric, such as cotton Lycra, to control the body's soft tissue from rib cage to hips. The garment can be made with one or more layers of Lycra to achieve the degree of compression desired. For garments with a high degree of compression, a bra back Hook-and-Eye tape with a single column of eyes can be used for a Center Front opening. The design for this garment was suggested by Susan Stacey of FabricDepotCo.com.

To create a Dream Shaper, use Press'n Seal to make a mold of the body from the rib cage to below the waist. Since stretch fabric is used for the body of this garment, the initial fitting must be done with the fabric for the finished garment. The top and bottom of the rib cage can be finished with plush Bra Band elastic and the neck with neckline elastic.

Qty	Basic Dream Shaper Materials
1 roll	Glad Press'n Seal
1 each	Masking tape, 2" (5 cm)
1	Marking Pen (i.e. Sharpie)
1 yd	Compression Fabric
2 yds	Bra Band Elastic, 3/4" (2 cm)
2 yds	3/8" Neckline Elastic (1 cm)
1/2 yd	Hook-and-Eye Tape (optional)

 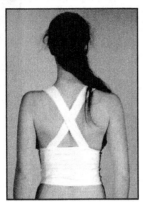

Basic X-Back Dream Shaper

 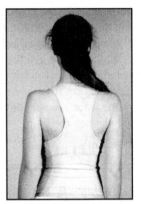

Front Opening Racerback Dream Shaper

I. Create a Mold of the Rib Cage

To create a mold, follow these steps.

1. From the rib cage to just above the pelvic bone, wrap Press'n Seal around the body, compressing any soft tissue.
2. After the rib cage is completely covered with Press'n Seal, apply masking tape.
3. On one side of the body, draw lines indicating the rib cage, waist, and hem from Center Front to Center Back.
4. Remove the mold from the body.

Note: Since this mold is created to compress the entire body, removing it may require some care. The spine tends to be slightly indented from the rest of the back, so cutting it open at Center Back is a good option. As only the side of half the body is used to create the pattern, another alternative is to carefully rip the side that will not used.

  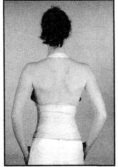

Wrapped Rib Cage

  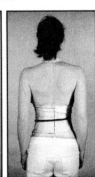

Design Lines

II. Convert the Mold to a Paper Pattern

Since this garment will be made in stretch fabric, the mold does not need to lay completely flat. The fabric will stretch to assume a three-dimensional shape.

1. Reinforce the inside of the mold with masking tape.
2. From the good side, cut the mold along the Center Front, Center Back, rib cage, and hem lines.
3. Add sewing notches at the side seam, then separate the front and back patterns along this seam.
4. Place the mold on a piece of pattern paper, then trace the front and back shapes.
5. Mark the Center Front and Center Back lines as fold lines.
6. To the top and bottom of the pattern, add 3/4" (2 cm) elastic allowances.
7. To add some tension to the fit, do not add seam allowances to the side seam, which will be sewn with a 1/2" (12 mm) seam allowance.

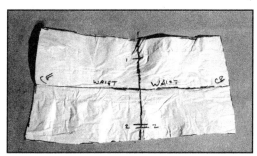
The Trimmed Mold

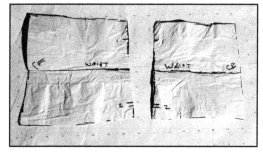
Trace the Mold

III. Sew a Trial Fitting Version

This garment must be cut from the final fabric for fitting. In this example, the Dream Shaper is made with the two-piece Princess Bust Sling Bra pattern (page 79) and the X-Back design (page 75). The Bust Sling Top should be underlined with a non-stretch fabric.

Note: Before cutting the fabric from the pattern, verify the Rib Cage fabric stretches enough to be pulled over the head or hips. To allow for fitting adjustments, sew with a 5 mm long by 1 mm wide zigzag basting stitch in Steps 4 and 6 below.

1. Use the patterns to cut the fabric for the Bust Sling Top and the Rib Cage section.
2. Use the patterns to cut the Bust Sling Top from the underlining material, then zigzag the underlining to the fashion fabric, wrong sides together.
3. Sew the Bust Sling Top as described on page 76.
4. Sew the side seams of the Rib Cage, good sides together, using a 1/2" (12 mm) seam allowance.
5. Pin the Bust Sling Top to the Rib Cage's Center Front. Adjust the position of the Bust Sling Top based on the 3/4" (2 cm) Rib Cage's elastic allowance and the 1/4" (6 mm) Bust Sling Top's seam allowance.
6. Sew the Bust Sling Top to the Rib Cage.

Pull Over Measurement
_____

IV. Fit the Dream Shaper

 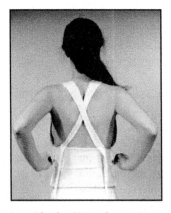 

1. Put the garment on the wearer, wrong side out, then verify the fit at the side seam.

2. Pin the X-Back straps to the top of the Rib Cage section.

3. Establish the length of the elastic for the hem.

Elastic for Hem
_____

4. Establish the length of the elastic for the rib cage.

Elastic for Rib Cage
_____

V. Finish the Dream Shaper

To finish the Dream Shaper after fitting adjustments have been completed, first separate the Bust Sling Top from the Rib Cage.

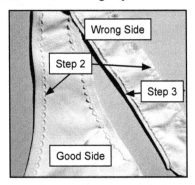 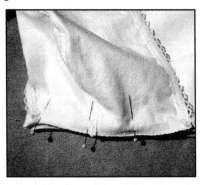 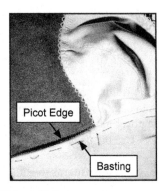

1. Remove the garment and, based on the fitting, adjust the patterns.
2. Use a 2 mm zigzag to sew the neckline edging elastic along the outside of the Bust Sling Top. This elastic should be sewn to the right side of the fashion fabric with the plush side up and the picot edge facing into the band.
3. Trim off the excess seam allowance.
4. Turn the elastic to the inside, then sew with a 4 mm zigzag stitch.

5. Pin the Bust Sling Top to the Rib Cage's Center Front, good sides together. Adjust the position of the Bust Sling Top based on the 3/4" (2 cm) elastic allowance of the Rib Cage and the 1/4" (6 mm) seam allowance of the Bust Sling Top.
6. Sew the Bust Sling Top to the Rib Cage.
7. Pin 3/4" (2 cm) plush back elastic to the good side of the Rib Cage's top edge. Sandwich the Bust Sling Top between the Rib Cage and the elastic. The plush side should be up with the picot edge facing toward the body of the rib cage. Sew close to the picot edge with a 2 mm zigzag stitch.

8. Trim off the excess seam allowance, then turn the elastic to the inside and hand baste in place. As you baste, align the picot edge so it just shows along the top of the Rib Cage.
9. Using a 4 mm or triple-step zigzag, topstitch the elastic, then remove the basting.
10. For the elastic along the bottom of the Rib Cage, repeat Steps 7 through 9.

Dream Shaper with Center Front Opening

A high degree of compression can be achieved by using multiple layers of fabric. This may necessitate creating a Center Front opening, which is also useful for people with mobility issues, and can be accomplished using hook-and-eye tape with a single column of eyes. This example uses a three-piece Princess Seam Top (page 79) and Racerback design (page 84).

I. Prepare the Dream Shaper for an Initial Fitting

1. Using the patterns, cut the fabric for the Bust Sling Top and the Rib Cage section.
2. Using the patterns, cut the underlining material for the Bust Sling Top, then zigzag it to the fashion fabric, wrong sides together.
3. Sew the Bust Sling Top's Princess seams.
4. To sew the Racerback to the Bust Sling Top, use a 5 mm long by 1 mm wide zigzag basting stitch.
5. To sew the Rib Cage's side seams, good sides together, use a 5 mm long by 1 mm wide zigzag basting stitch and 1/2" (12 mm) seam allowance.
6. Based on the 3/4" (2 cm) Rib Cage's elastic allowance and the 1/4" (6 mm) Bust Sling Top's seam allowance, adjust the position of the Bust Sling Top and then pin it to the Rib Cage's Center Front.
7. Sew the Bust Sling Top to the Rib Cage.
8. Verify the fit.
9. Separate the Bust Sling Top from the Rib Cage, then adjust the patterns as necessary.

II. Sew the Hook-and-Eye Tape

To add the hook-and-eye tape, separate the front of the Rib Cage into two pieces along the Center Front line. To sew hook-and-eye tape, sandwich the fashion fabric between the two edges of the tape.

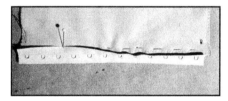  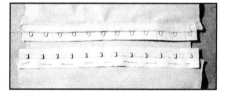

1. Cut the Rib Cage's front panel into two at Center Front.
2. Align the Rib Cage's Center Front edge to the center of the hook-and-eye tape's inside, then hand baste.
3. Using a 2 mm straight stitch, sew the tape to the wrong side of the Rib Cage's front.

4. Fold the eye tape's fashion side over the Rib Cage's good side, then sew in place.

5. Align the Rib Cage's Center Front edge to the center of the eye-tape's inside, then hand baste.
6. Sew the eye tape's fashion side to the good side of the Rib Cage's front.

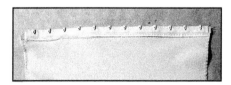

7. Fold the inside of the hook closure to the wrong side of the Rib Cage, then sew in place.

III. Finish the Dream Shaper

The Rib Cage section can now be sewn back onto the Bust Sling Top.

1. Sew the Rib Cage's side seams, good sides together.
2. Sew neckline elastic to the Bust Sling Top's inside edge.
3. Sew the Racerback's side seam to the Bust Sling's side.
4. Sew neckline elastic around the two armholes.
5. Pin the Bust Sling's Center Front to the Rib Cage, then sew the Bust Sling Top to the Rib Cage.
6. Sew elastic to the bottom of the Rib Cage section.

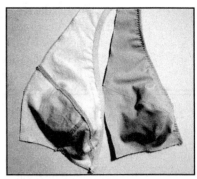

Neckline Elastic

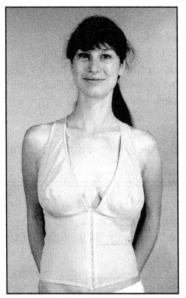 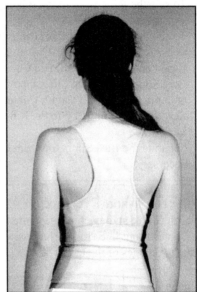

Finished Front Opening Dream Shaper

Leotards and One-Piece Swimsuits

One-piece swimsuits and leotards can be created by connecting Bust Sling Tops to Fitted Briefs (page 42). A pattern extending from the waistline up to the rib cage can be made from the Dream Shaper patterns or by taking the body's measurements.

Important Note: The fabric for these garments must be 4-way stretch, meaning it must stretch both across the width and along the length. Lycra is a good choice for swimsuits because of its tolerance for sunlight, salt water, and chlorine.

Creating a Fitted Briefs Pattern Extension

To make patterns from a Dream Shaper, follow these steps:
1. Put on a version of the Dream Shaper that has been fitted.
2. Put on a High Rise Fitted Briefs.
3. The Dream Shaper extends to the pelvic bone which is below the Fitted Briefs' top. Pull the Fitted Briefs over the Dream Shaper and mark the location of the Fitted Briefs waistline on the Dream Shaper.
4. Use these marks to create the pattern.

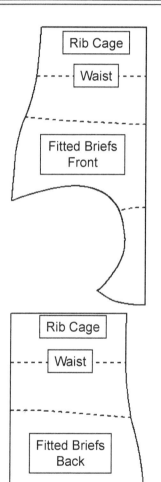

 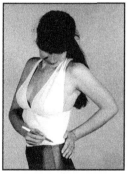

To make patterns from measurements, follow these steps:
1. Put on a version of the Fitted Briefs.
2. Measure the circumference of the rib cage.
3. Measure the distance from the rib cage to the top of the Fitted Briefs.
4. On copies of the Fitted Briefs patterns, extend the Center Front and Center Back lines by the amount in Step 3, then draw in a horizontal line for the rib cage.
5. On the front and back patterns, mark off 1/4 the rib cage circumference measurement on the rib cage line, then connect the end of the rib cage line down to the waist line.

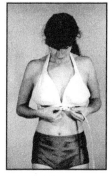 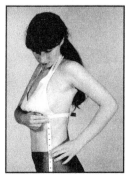

Rib Cage – Inhale: _____

Rib Cage to Waistband: _____

Sewing the Finished Garment

The techniques for sewing a finished garment will depend on the specific look desired. For this example, a swimsuit ring is used with the halter neck pattern, and sliders are added to the rib cage's elastic in the back so that elastic cording can be used. The Bust Sling Top is underlined with non-stretch fabric.

1. Using the patterns, cut the fabric.
2. Zigzag the underlining to the Bust Sling Top's pieces.
3. Pin, then sew the shoulder, Princess, and side seams using a 1 mm zigzag stitch.
4. Press open the sewn seams, then use a 2 mm zigzag to topstitch the seam allowances. Trim off any excess seam allowance.
5. On the wrong side of the fabric, pin 1/4" (6 mm) elastic around the Bust Sling Top and the leg openings.
6. Use a 3 mm zigzag stitch to sew the elastic to the fashion fabric, then turn the elastic and zigzag in place.
7. Cut the rib cage elastic to the length established on page 102 plus 1" (2.5 cm).
8. Pin the rib cage elastic in a loop with a 1" (2.5 cm) overlap.
9. Use a 1 mm long, 4 mm wide zigzag stitch to sew the elastic closed.
10. Pin the elastic to the wrong side of the rib cage's edge, sandwiching the Bust Sling Top between the rib cage and the elastic.
11. Use a 2 mm wide zigzag stitch to sew the elastic's top edge, stretching as necessary.
12. Use a zigzag stitch to sew the bottom of the elastic.
13. Turn the elastic to the inside of the garment, then sew a 4 mm or decorative zigzag along the bottom edge of the elastic.
14. Put pins along the back of the rib cage elastic 1-1/2", 3", and 4.5" (40, 80, and 12 cm) from Center Back.
15. At the pin locations, hand sew 3/8" bra sliders to the rib cage elastic.
16. Thread elastic cording through the sliders. This cording can be adjusted in a fitting.

An alternative to elastic cording would be using 1/4" (6 mm) elastic to create fashion fabric straps as described on page 95.

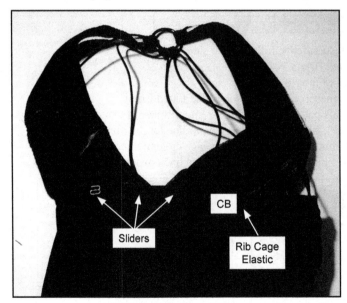

Finished Swimsuit Top

Conventional Bras

This section shows how to make conventional bras from a Bra Sloper pattern. The initial pattern can be changed to achieve diverse designs. Variations of a Bra Sloper can also be created for specific shapes such as pushup bras and 50's style bullet bras. This means it is possible to have a Bra Sloper for everyday wear, another for special occasion evening clothes, and another for active sports.

The amount of shaping and support depends on both the size and age of the breasts. These instructions include three different ways of establishing breast shape for a Bra Sloper cup: wear a bra that fits well; use the natural shape of the body; or use Press'n Seal and masking tape to sculpt the shape of the breast.

The instructions have been written so Slopers can be created for one's self (DIY). Nonetheless, some steps are easier to follow with a helping hand.

Muslin Sloper

Lace Bra

Bullet Bra with Matching Bra Form

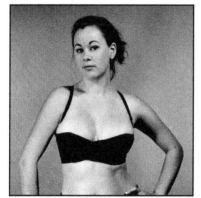

Balconette Bra

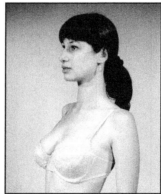

Push Up Bra

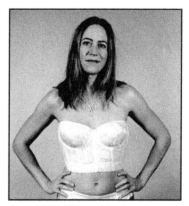

Strapless, Low-Back Bra

An Overview of the Process

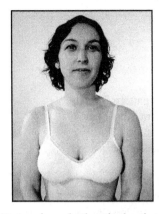

1. Determine whether the bra is to be shaped using an existing bra (page 115), natural posture (page 117), or Press'n Seal (page 118).

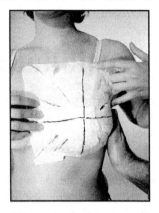

2. Create a mold of the Bra Sloper on the body (page 114).

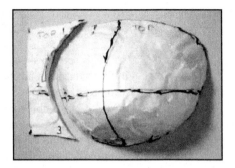

3. Remove the three-dimensional mold from the body.

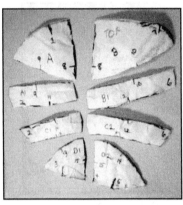

4. Trim the mold, then cut it into flat pattern pieces (page 119).

5. Create a test muslin sloper and adjust the fit as necessary (page 121).

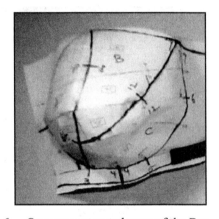

6. On a reconstructed copy of the Bra Sloper, create the design for a bra (page 124).

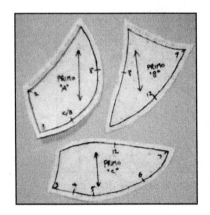

7. Make a pattern for the new bra design and cut a test version in muslin (page 125).

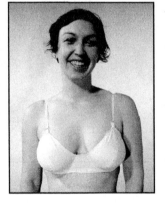

8. Test the fit of the new design and adjust as necessary.

9. Sew the finished bra (page 130).

Design Considerations

Parts of a Conventional Bra

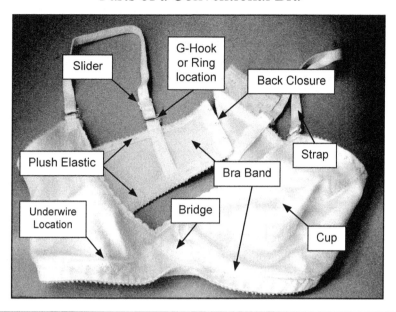

Reference Lines

To create a Custom Bra Sloper, use the vertical and horizontal reference lines shown below, including Center Front (CF), Above Bust, Bust, and the Rib Cage. Two additional vertical reference lines are the Apex Center and Side. The Apex Center line is parallel to Center Front. It is located at the apex of the bust. The Side line is located where the bust merges with the rib cage in front of the arm.

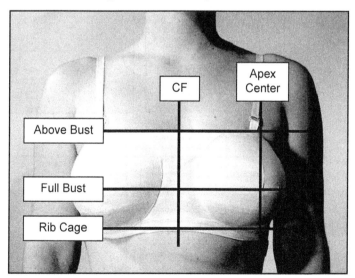
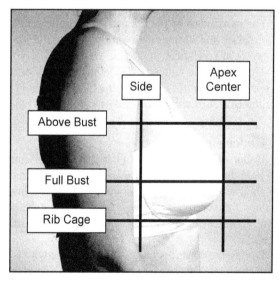

Factors that Affect the Fit of a Conventional Bra

Pattern Shapes

The shapes of custom-fit patterns vary. No two bodies are the same and sometimes surprising shapes emerge. Believe the shapes derived from the body.

The photo to the right shows the shape of the masking tape molds for the Back Band of two people. This Back Band is the shape of the body derived from putting strips of Velcro around the body just above and below the bust. It goes from the edge of the Bra Cup to Center Back. As you can see, one Back Band is relatively straight and the other is distinctly curved. But both shapes result in a Back Band that is parallel to the floor when on the body.

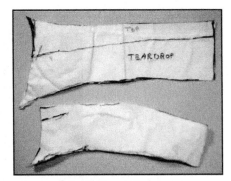

Back Band Shapes
From Two People

Fabric Grain Lines

With these instructions, bras can be made from either woven or knit fabric.

For Bra Cups in woven fabric, the grain lines should follow as closely as possible the Apex Center and Bust lines described on page 109.

Bra Back Bands need to have some stretch so the Underlining should be a stretch fabric such as powerknit or powernet, which can be covered with woven fashion fabric cut on the bias.

For knits, the direction of stretch should be at a 45 degree angle to the grain lines of woven fabric.

 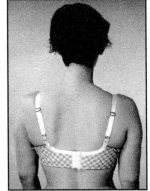

Woven versus Knit Fabric

The two photos on the right show the same pattern cut in a woven fabric and a knit: the first from muslin, the second from two layers of knit Tricot.

The main issue with knits is that there is less stretch along the seam lines than for the rest of the fabric. To avoid this, interline Bra Cups with a woven fabric or a stabilizer.

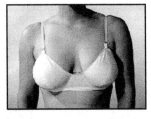 

Underwires

Underwires add control to a bra's shape. A primary function is to hold the bridge close to the chest wall as shown in these two photos. Shaping from underwires can add to a bra's comfort, but only if the correct wire size is used. Fortunately, online bra supply resources offer a variety of different underwire sizes and shapes.

During the construction process, the underwire is added as one of the final steps so you can easily determine at that time whether to include an underwire for a given design.

Some women may have one breast a different size from the other. This can be determined by testing with different size underwires.

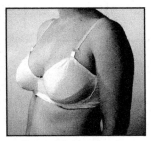 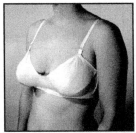

Bra with Underwire   Bra with No Underwire

Back Band Height

Bras can be supported by both the Back Band and Shoulder Straps. The consensus of opinion is that shoulder straps should carry no more than 10% of the breasts' weight. Straps carrying too much weight can cause problems with the arms and lower back. This means the Back Band must support the majority of the weight. To achieve this, the top of the bra's back should be kept close to the Bust line.

The photos to the right show what happens when the upper edge of the back bra band is dropped too low. The breast, instead of being lifted, starts to sag, as shown by the black lines. The tendency for the wearer would be to lift the breasts using the Shoulder Straps. The larger the breasts, the more this becomes a problem.

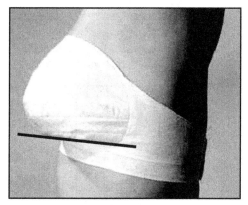 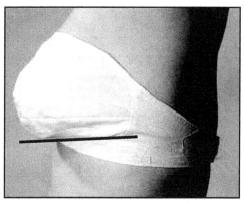

| Bra with 3 Rows of Hook-and-Eye Closure | Bra with 2 Rows of Hook-and-Eye Closure |

Bridge Width

The width of the Bridge between Bra Cups will control the distance between Apex Center lines. However, if the Bridge is too small, it can cause underwires to dig into the sides of the breasts.

Fortunately, the width of the Bridge is easy to adjust by leaving a Center Front seam when making a muslin trial version for a bra design. For the sloper indicated, the photo on the far right illustrates the design offering optimum shaping and comfort.

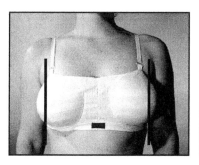 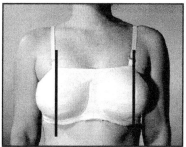 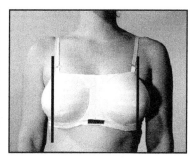

Rib Cage Expansion

The rib cage increases and decreases in size during breathing. This means that the Back Band must use fabric, such as powernet, that stretches. The powernet can be covered with woven fashion fabric by either cutting the fashion fabric on the bias, or cutting it long enough that it gathers slightly when the powernet is in its relaxed state.

To verify there is adequate allowance for breathing, record the size of the rib cage while inhaling deeply, then while exhaling deeply.

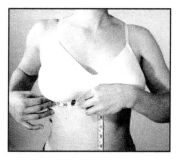

Inhale	Exhale

Materials and Tools

Bras require special materials and specific notions or "bra findings." Before you create patterns for a bra you should acquire the bra findings, so you can adjust your patterns accordingly. For example, bra straps come in different widths. The rings and sliders for these straps need to be the same size as the straps.

Qty	Material for Molds & Muslin Trial Bras
1	Box of Glad's Press'n Seal (optional)
½ yd	Muslin
1 yd	Paper Towels
1 roll	2" Masking Tape
1 roll	3/4" Masking Tape
2 yds	Bias Tape
3	3/4" Bra Strap Rings
3 yds	Velcro
1 yd	12 or 14 gauge solid copper wire*
1	Sheet of Posterboard
1	G-hook for front closing (optional)

* Solid copper wire, used by electricians, is best because it is easy to bend yet retains the shape desired. Stranded copper wire does not work.

Press'n Seal for Bra Molds

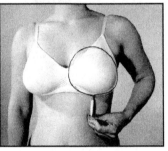

Solid Copper Wire
for Underwire Size

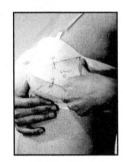

Posterboard
for Cup Design

Material for a Bra			
½ yd	Fabric for the Bra Cup (Woven or knit)	½ yd	Powernet for the Back Band
2 yds	Bra Strap Elastic (3/8", 1/2", 5/8", or 3/4")	½ yd	Neckline Edging Elastic
2 to 4	Bra Strap Sliders (3/8", 1/2", 5/8", or 3/4")	6"	Hook-and-Eye Tape
2 to 4	Bra Strap Rings (3/8", 1/2", 5/8", or 3/4")	1 yd	Underwire Casing
1 yd	3/8" (10 mm) plush elastic for top of Bra Band	1 pair	Underwire, see page 113
1 yd	1/2" or 3/4" plush elastic for bottom of Bra Band	1	Front closing (optional)

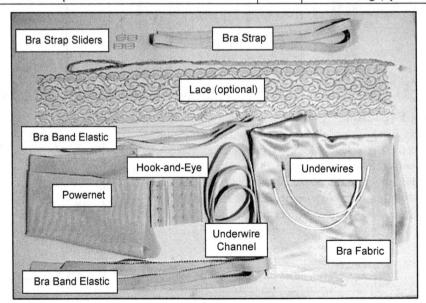

Underwires

Underwires can be used to control the shape of a bra. They are also useful for determining seam lines while creating a Bra Cup mold.

To determine the size of the underwire needed, use a length of copper wire to establish where the breast meets the rib cage, as shown in the photo. Then compare the shape of the copper wire to the chart below.

This chart shows the inside edge of the underwires offered by various online suppliers. The dimension is based on the size of the underwire for a B Cup bra.

The actual size, shape, and length of the underwires can vary from one manufacturer to the next so this chart is an approximation. Some of these suppliers offer charts that can be downloaded to determine the order number and exact size of the underwires offered. When first ordering from a company, it is always best to purchase a size larger and a size smaller as well as the size you think is needed.

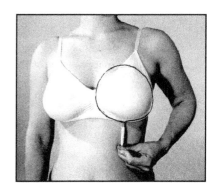

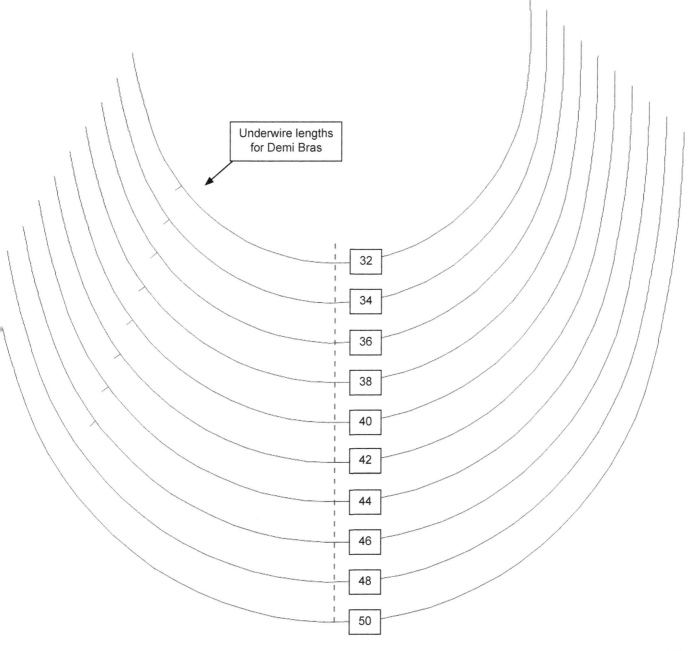

Underwire lengths for Demi Bras

32
34
36
38
40
42
44
46
48
50

Creating a Bra Sloper Mold

The instructions in this section describe three different ways to create a Bra Sloper: over a bra, over a horizontal body, or with Press'n Seal. The first two procedures utilize a paper towel for the Bra Cup mold's inside layer.

Paper Towel for Bra Cup Mold

Use the pattern below to prepare a paper towel.
1. Make a copy of the pattern below.
2. Place a paper towel over the copy.
3. Put 3/4" (2 cm) masking tape on the towel over the Bust and Apex Center lines to reinforce them.
4. Draw the Full Bust and Apex Center lines onto the masking tape.
5. Mark the Center Front (CF), Top, Side, and Rib Cage locations on the towel.
6. Cut the towel along the dotted lines.

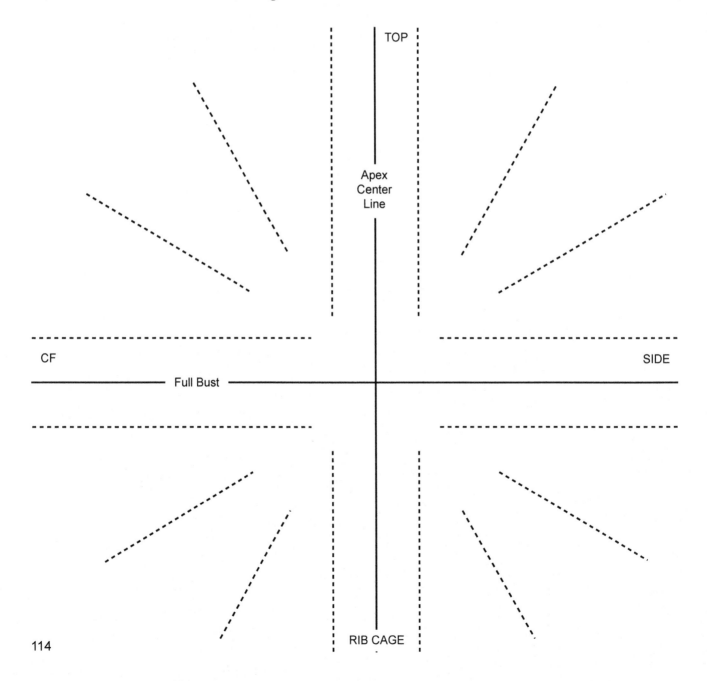

Creating a Sloper Mold Over an Existing Bra

To sculpt the sloper shape, create a mold that captures the shape of the body from just above the breast down to the rib cage. Some women may have one breast larger than the other. Make the mold for the larger breast. The Bra Cup can then be reduced for the smaller during fitting and sewing.

Step I. Mold the Towel to the Breast.

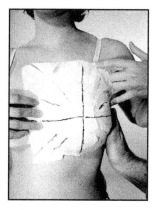 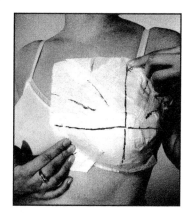 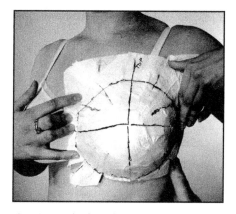

1. Place the towel over the breast.
2. Adjust the Bust and Apex Center lines to the correct position.
3. Adjust the towel to cover the breast as smoothly as possible.

4. To create a mold of the breast, secure masking tape over the towel. First, tape the top of the bust just enough to hold the towel in place, then tape under the bust, lifting to shape as required.
5. Tape the towel at Center Front along the breast bone for the bridge.

6. Draw the location around the bust where it meets the chest wall. Use underwire or copper wire to draw this shape.
7. Draw in the Center Front line and the top and bottom of the bra bridge.

Step II. Add a Back Band.

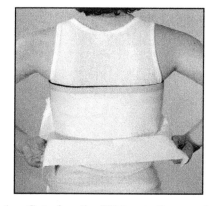 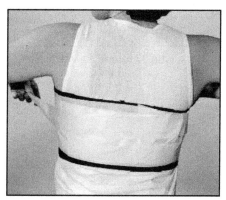 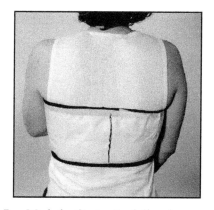

1. Cut a length of Velcro to fit around the Above Bust.
2. Cut a length of Velcro to fit around the Rib Cage.
3. Tape paper towels along the length of the Above Bust Velcro.
4. Fasten the Above Bust Velcro around the body.

5. Fasten the Rib Cage Velcro around the body so that it holds the towel for the Bra Band in place.
6. Tape the towel around the body so that it conforms to the contours of the back.

7. Mark the Center Back line down the spine. If you are fitting yourself, mark the top and bottom of Center Back at the spine, then draw the line after the towel has been removed.

Step III. Mark Reference Locations on the Bra Mold.

Before removing the mold, draw lines and sewing notches to record where the contours of the body change the shape of the mold. Number the sewing notches. The mold can then be trimmed to verify fit.

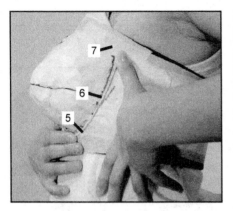 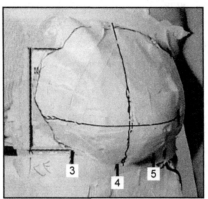 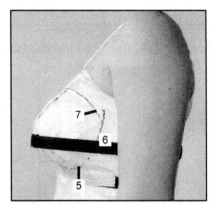

1. Mark the side of the Bra Cup on the Bra Band towel. Use the underwire to draw this shape.
2. On the Bra Cup, mark the top (#7), Full Bust (#6), and bottom of the Bra Band (#5).

3. Put masking tape over the Rib Cage Velcro and mark the Center Front (CF), side of the Bridge (#3), bust Apex line (#4), and side of the Cup (#5).

4. Use a length of Velcro to draw the full bust line from Center Front to Center Back. Mark this as #6.
5. Remove the sloper, trim the Bra Cup to the seam lines, then verify the fit.

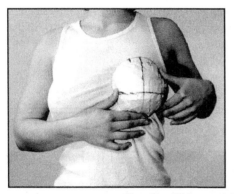 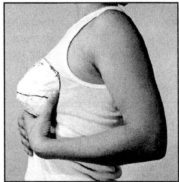

Bra Cup Trimmed to Verify Fit

Creating a Sloper Mold Over the Natural Body

A Bra Sloper mold can be created from the body in its natural state without any supporting device such as a bra. If you are creating a sloper for a small breast that is self-supporting, standing naturally in an upright position might be all that is required. Another option is to lie down flat so that the breasts are naturally compressed. This would be a good way to create a sports bra where movement during strenuous exercise should be minimized. The photos below show the difference between a Bra Sloper created when the body is horizontal as opposed to one created over an existing bra.

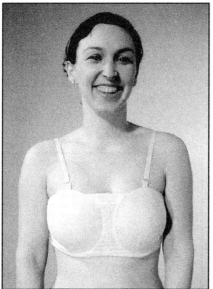 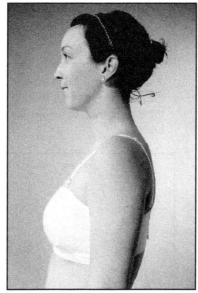 

Sloper from Mold Created While Lying Down   Sloper Created Using a Bra

Creating the Mold

To shape the mold, the person being fitted can either be naked or wear a close fitting garment such as a tank top. Follow the same sequence of steps for creating a mold over an existing bra as described on page 115.

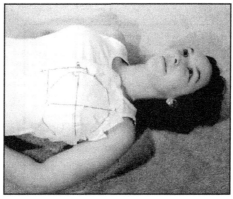

Bra Cup Mold made while lying down

Creating a Sloper Mold Using Press'n Seal

Press'n Seal is strong enough to support large breasts while a Bra Sloper Mold is created.

Start by covering the rib cage. This provides a surface to anchor the Press'n Seal used to sculpt a breast's soft tissue.

In addition to providing support, the Press'n Seal offers a protective layer on the skin when masking tape is added to stabilize the shape.

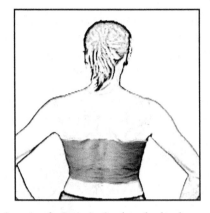

1. Apply Press'n Seal to the back so that it covers the area from above the bust in front to below the breasts.

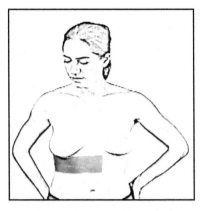

2. Apply Press'n Seal on the rib cage below the breast.

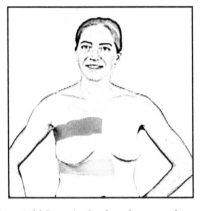

3. Add Press'n Seal to the area above the bust.

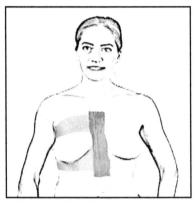

4. Apply Press'n Seal to Center Front between the breasts.

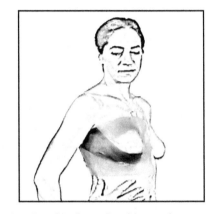

5. Starting from the side, apply Press'n Seal lifting the underside to sculpt the breast tissue into the desired shape.

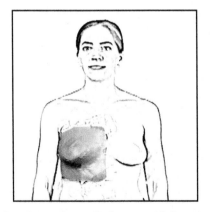

6. Cover the entire breast with Press'n Seal, then cover the Press'n Seal with masking tape.

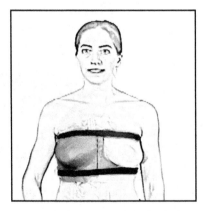

7. Place Velcro around the body just above the breast, then draw a line from Center Front to Center Back.
8. Place Velcro around the body just below the breast, then draw a line from Center Front to Center Back.

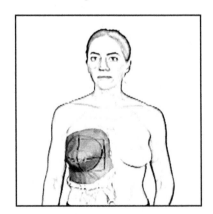

9. Draw in the Center Back line.
10. Use an underwire to indicate where the breast tissue meets the rib cage.
11. Draw the Apex and Full Bust lines.
12. Remove the mold.

Creating a Bra Sloper from a Mold

The Sloper pattern is created from the molds for the Back Band, Bra Cup, and Bridge. The idea is to change the mold from a three-dimensional shape to a two-dimensional shape that reflects the wearer's body. The Sloper can then be fitted to refine the shape if necessary. Once the shape is finalized, it may be used to either create a bra or as a base to design other bra patterns.

The Back Bra Band and Bridge molds should already be flat shapes. The Bra Cup will need to be divided into several pattern pieces so each piece will lay flat. The individual pieces vary depending on the exact shape of the Bra Cup. Adjustments can always be made later during the fitting process.

It is a good idea to date the patterns. If you are creating slopers for different shapes, name each one to avoid confusion.

Step I. The Back Bra Band Pattern

The pattern for the Back Bra Band includes the side joined to the Bra Cup, the bottom of the above bust Velcro, Center Back, and the top of the rib cage Velcro.

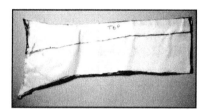

1. Lay the Back Bra Band flat.
2. Draw the top of the Bra Band along the lower edge of the upper bust Velcro. It should be a straight line.
3. Mark this line "TOP."
4. Draw the bottom of the Bra Band along the upper edge of the rib cage Velcro. Depending on the shape of the wearer, this line may be curved.
5. Remove the Velcro and trace the shape onto a sheet of pattern paper.
6. Mark the Bra Cup bottom, bust, and top locations 5, 6, and 7 respectively.
7. Add a 3/4" (2 cm) overlap at Center Back.
8. Add 1/4" (6 mm) seam allowances to all other seams.

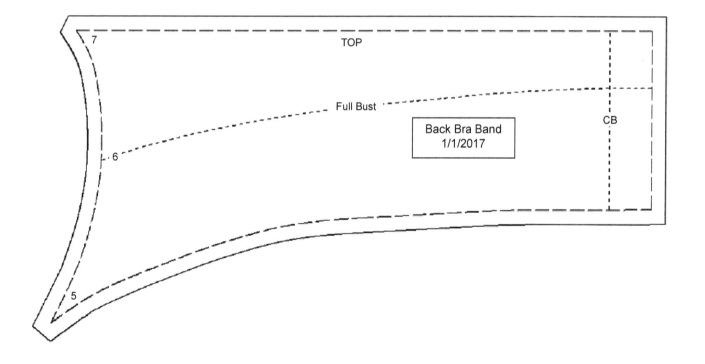

Step II. Prepare the Bra Cup and Bridge Pattern

The three-dimensional mold of the bust from Center Front to the side of the breast must be changed into two-dimensional patterns.

1. If necessary, redraw the lines established during the fitting, including the Full Bust and Apex lines.
2. Mark sewing notches where the Bra Cup meets the top, Full Bust, and bottom of the Bridge.
3. Mark the top of the Bridge #1.
4. Mark the Bust line on the Bridge #2.
5. Mark where the bottom of the Bra Cup meets the Bridge #3.
6. Turn the Bra Cup mold over and reinforce the shape from the inside with masking tape.
7. Cut the Bridge from the Bra Cup and trace the shape onto pattern paper.

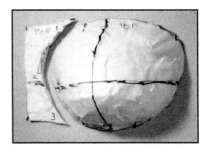

Trimmed Bridge and Bra Cup

Step III. Create the Bra Cup Pattern

The Bra Cup mold must now be cut into pieces until each piece lies flat. Mark sewing notches on each pattern piece. Use the Full Bust and Apex lines as the fabric grain lines.

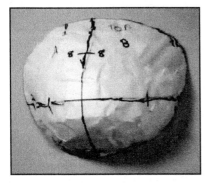

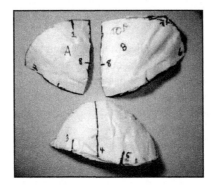

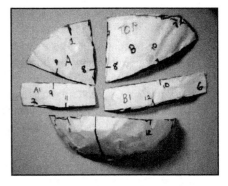

1. Label the top inside quadrant of the Bra Cup "A" and the top outside quadrant "B".
2. Add a sewing notch on the Apex line and mark it #8.

3. Mark the bottom of the Apex line #4.
4. Mark the sewing notches where the Bra Cup meets the Back Band at the bottom #5, Full Bust #6, and top #7.
5. Add sewing notches on the Full Bust line.
6. Cut the "A" and "B" quadrants from the Bra Cup.

7. If either of the two top quadrants is not laying flat, draw additional seam lines, mark them "A1" and "B1" respectively, then add sewing notches and number them. Cut off the lower portions.

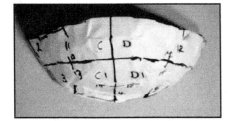

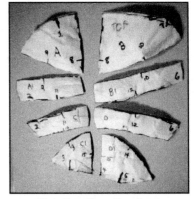

8. On the bottom of the Bra Cup, draw a line below the Full Bust line following the contour of the Bra Cup.
9. Label the sections on both sides of the Apex line C, C1, D, D1, etc.

10. Mark sewing notches on all the pattern pieces and number them.
11. Separate the Bra Cup and make sure all the individual pieces lay as flat as possible.

The Bra Cup Sections

120

Step IV. Create a Rib Cage Band Pattern

During fitting, the locations for the Center Front, bridge, and Bra Cup are marked on a piece of masking tape attached to the rib cage Velcro. These marks should be recorded on a paper pattern as #3, #4, and #5 respectively.

1. Trace the rib cage pattern onto a sheet of pattern paper.
2. Verify that the distance from sewing notch #5 to the CB is the same length as the bottom seam.
3. Add 3/4" (2 cm) to the Center Back for a Velcro back closure.
4. Add a 1/2" (12 mm) seam allowance to the Center Front and 1/4" (6 mm) to the top and bottom.

CF   3   4   5   Rib Cage Band 1/1/2017   CB

Preparing to Sew a Muslin Sloper for Fitting

It is important to verify the fit of the sloper using a fabric such as muslin. When you are sewing the Bra Cup, the position of each piece is critical. Carefully following all the steps below will help ensure the success of your efforts.

Poster Board Trial

1. Trace the Bra Cup's sewing lines onto stiff paper such as poster board, then cut. Only one Bra Cup needs to be tested.
2. Using the sewing notches as primary reference points, tape the poster board pieces together.
3. If the edges of the Bra Cup pieces come out slightly different lengths, trim them as necessary to create smooth continuous seams.
4. Verify the poster board Bra Cup is the shape desired.
5. Separate the poster board back to individual pattern pieces.
6. Transfer any adjustments back to the paper pattern.

Sewing the Bra Cup

The shapes of a Bra Cup's pattern pieces can be confusingly similar. Adequate sewing notches help as does carefully labeling the fabric. When marking fashion fabric, use a Mark B Gone pen. When marking muslin for a trial sloper, however, you can use permanent ink.

To ensure a left and right side, develop a consistent sequence of steps when sewing Bra Cups. Always begin by sewing seams that dead end into another seam.

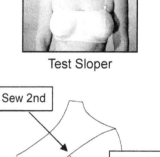

Test Sloper

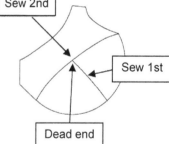

1. Keep the paper patterns pinned to the fabric until just before you are ready to sew that portion of the Bra Cup.

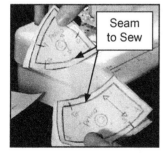

2. Remove a pattern piece and immediately flip one of the fabric pieces to create a left and right side.

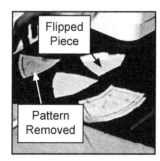

3. Repeat Step 2 with the next portion of the Bra Cup to be sewn. The fabric is now laid out with a top and bottom aligned along the seam to be sewn.

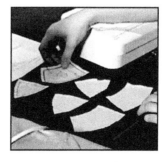

4. Flip the bottom over the top along the seam and immediately put a pin through the seam to be sewn.

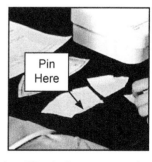

Sewing a Muslin Sloper for Fitting

Sew with straight stitches to allow for adjustments.

1. As illustrated on page 120, trace the Bra Cup sections, including sewing notches, onto a sheet of paper, then add 1/4" (6 mm) seam allowances. For the direction of the grain, use the Apex and Full Bust lines.
2. Trace the Bridge onto a sheet of pattern paper. Make the Center Front a seam with a 1/2" (12 mm) seam allowance, then add 1/4" (6 mm) seam allowances to the Bridge pattern.
3. On a copy of the Bra Specification sheet on page 141, record the sequence of steps for sewing the sloper.
4. Pin the pattern pieces to muslin, then cut them out but leave them pinned.
5. Sew the Bra Cup pieces, then press open.
6. Sew the Bra Cup to the bridge, then press open.
7. Sew the Bra Cup to the back bra band, then press open.
8. Sew the rib cage band to the bra, then press open.
9. Sew a line of stay stitching around the outside edges of the bra.
10. Press under the bra's outside edges along the stay stitching from Step 9, then topstitch in place.
11. If you are using a Center Front closing, add G-hooks to the right side of the bridge and loops of bias tape to the left.
12. If you are not using a Center Front closing, sew the Center Front seam, then press open.
13. Sew Velcro for a Center Back closure.
14. To test an underwire sloper, topstitch underwire channeling around the outside of the Bra Cup seam, then insert the underwire.
15. If necessary, add bias tape for bra straps. The bias tape bra strap should be sewn just to the outside of the Sloper's vertical Apex seam.

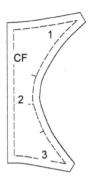

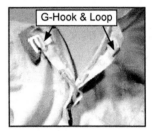

Center Front closing

Fitting the Sloper

For fit, some adjustments to the sloper may be required. The photo shows a trial muslin sloper created with the person lying down. The exposed seam allowances make it easy to adjust the fit of the Bra Cup.

Adjusting Bra Cup Size

If the wearer's breasts are different sizes, create the initial mold for the larger. To reduce the sewn Bra Cup one size, run a line of stay stitching 1/4" (6 mm) on the underwire seam allowance, then trim off the fabric along this stay stitching.

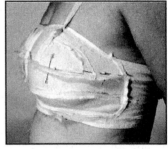

Fitting the Sloper

Example of a Completed Pattern

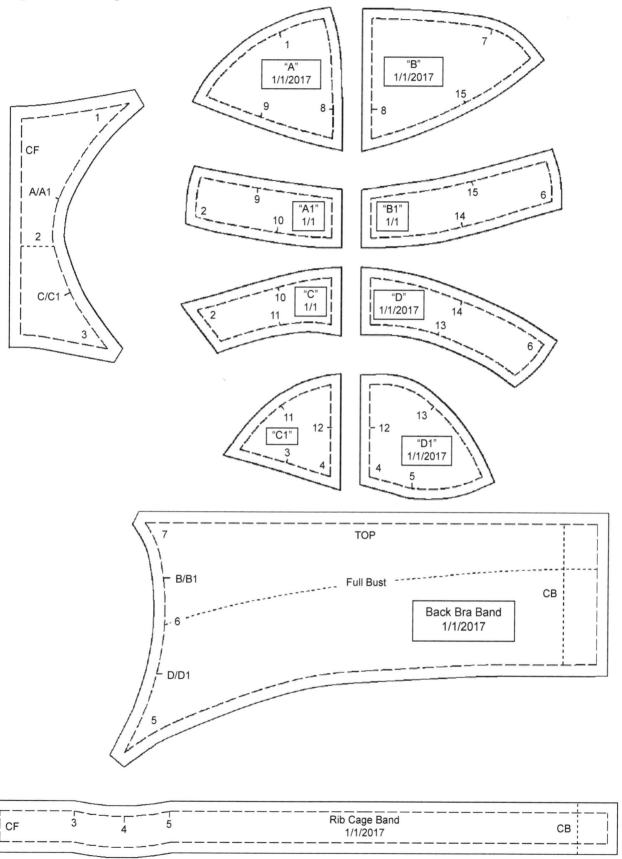

Creating a Pattern for a Bra Design

A Sloper can be used to create a variety of bra designs as illustrated. This chapter provides instructions for some basic variations. More designs are on page 136.

To create a bra design variation, first tape together a copy of the patterns along the sewing lines to reconstruct the bra as a three-dimensional shape. This can best be accomplished with poster board which is slightly stiff and holds a three-dimensional shape well. Typing paper can also be used. Next, draw design lines for the bra desired on this paper. Then cut along the new design lines to change the bra back to flat pattern pieces that can be cut from fabric.

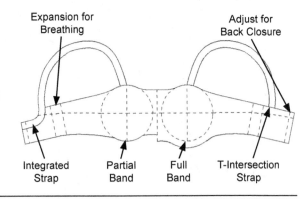

Step I. Record the Design Specifications

A Bra Cup is made using different pattern pieces. Some shapes may be very similar. To keep track of how the bra is to be assembled, record the process on a copy of the Bra Specification sheet, see page 141. For an example of how this sheet can be completed, see page 129

When creating a design, record which pattern piece must be sewn first. If one seam dead ends into another, that seam should be sewn first. For this example, the seam that joins "B" to "C" dead ends in "A". Therefore "B" should be sewn to "C" before the combined "B/C" pieces are sewn to "A".

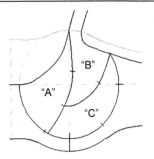

Step II. Create the Bra Design

Determining where seams are located for a Bra Cup is a judgment call. It is partly a matter of appearance and partly a matter of shaping and support. For shaping, at least one seam should pass through the Apex.

Note: The breast is soft tissue so when the pattern pieces for the bra design do not lie perfectly flat, the breast adjusts to the new shape. To verify the fit of a bra design, test the new pattern shapes with muslin before sewing the final bra.

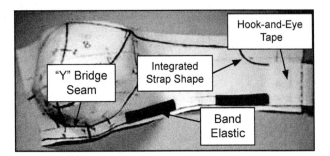

Full Band, "Y" Bridge, & Integrated Strap

1. Make a copy of the Bra Sloper.
2. Cut out the pieces along the sewing lines.
3. Tape together the pattern pieces to recreate the three-dimensional shape of the bra.
4. Draw the desired design.
5. For Full Band bras, draw the width of the bottom band elastic plus 1/8" (2 mm).

6. Mark sewing notches along the design lines including the new seam intersections, then cut along the design lines.
7. Adjust the height of the Back Band to correspond to the number of rows of hook-and-eyes used.

Partial Band Bras

For Partial Band bras, expand the Bra Cup shape by adding 1/4" (6 mm) to the sloper underwire seam at the bridge, rib cage band, and Back Band.

To convert a Partial Band to a front closing bra, see page 125.

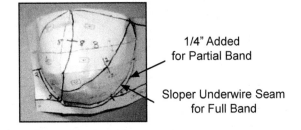

Step III. Create the Bra Cup Patterns

The Bra Cup pattern pieces can now be drawn by tracing the design lines from the reconstructed sloper. The pieces from the design may not lie completely flat as you trace them. The breast is soft tissue and adjusts to different shaped bras. Verify the fit of the new design with a trial muslin bra. Select a name for the bra design and write it on the pattern pieces.

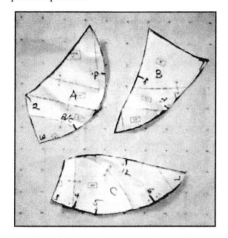

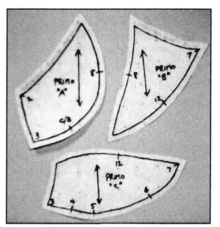

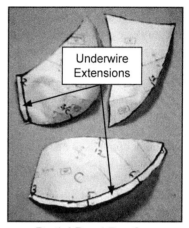

Partial Band Bra Cup
Expanded for Underwires

1. Cut the Bra Cup apart along the design lines.
2. Trace the shapes of the new pattern pieces on a new sheet of paper.
3. Use the vertical Apex Center and horizontal Bust lines to establish the grain of the fabric.
4. Mark the sewing notches on the bra pattern pieces.
5. Include notches where the seams intersect.
6. Add seam allowances to the neckline and underarm seam. These seam allowances should be the width of the elastics being used.
7. Add 1/4" (6 mm) seam allowances to the remaining seams.
8. Cut out the pattern pieces.

Modification for Front Closing Bras

To change a bra for a front closing device, tape the Bridge to the Bra Cup as shown.

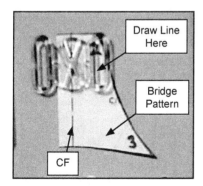

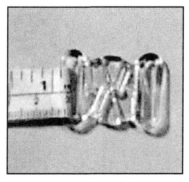

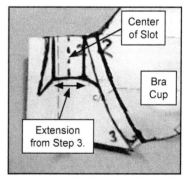

1. Center the front closing device over the Center Front line of the Bridge pattern.
2. Draw a line through the slot closest to the Bra Cup.
3. Use a tape measure to determine how much fabric will be required to secure the front closing device.
4. Add this width to the pattern.
5. Matching the slot lines, fold then trace the Bridge.
6. Tape the Bridge pattern to the Bra Cup.

Step IV. Create the Centerpiece Pattern

There are three basic types of Bridge patterns.

- A Partial Band Bra uses the Bridge, or a portion of it, for the Centerpiece pattern. Note: This type of bra must use underwires.
- The "Y" Centerpiece combines the Bridge and Rib Cage Band from the sloper into a shape that stops under the Bra Cup, typically at the Apex line.. The bottom of this Centerpiece may either be shaped or straight. The Back Band is extended under the Bra Cup to connect with the "Y" Centerpiece. The seam that joins the Centerpiece with the Back Band can be positioned to align with a Bra Cup seam during the design process.
- The Extended Centerpiece combines the Bridge, Rib Cage Band, and a short section of the Back Band. The Back Band is shortened accordingly.

Another option is to merge the Bridge into the Bra Cups to create an Integrated Bridge.

1. Trace the shape of the Centerpiece design on a new sheet of paper.
2. For "Y" and Extended Centerpiece patterns, straighten the Center Front line. This will be a fold line.
3. Add a seam allowance to the bottom of the Centerpiece that is equal to the width of the bottom band elastic plus 1/8" (3 mm).
4. Add 1/4" (6 mm) seam allowances to the remainder of the Centerpiece pattern.

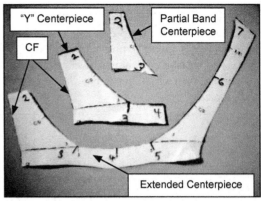

Pattern Shapes cut from Sloper Design Lines

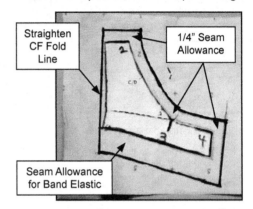

Variations for Front Closing Bras

To create a front closing bra, change the Center Front line of the Centerpiece to accommodate the type of closing device used.

These bras may utilize one or more of the front closing devices shown in the photo to the right; a column of hook-and-eye tape similar to the one used for a back closure; or a G-Hook.

- To add one or more front closing device(s) to a Centerpiece, follow the instructions on page 125.
- To add a column of hook-and-eyes to a Centerpiece, trim back the Center Front line to accommodate for the hook-and-eye tape.
- To add G-Hooks, add a 1/4" (6 mm) seam allowance to Center Front.

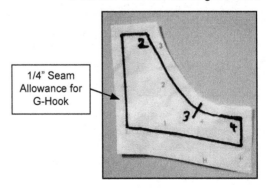

G-Hooks & Front Closing Devices

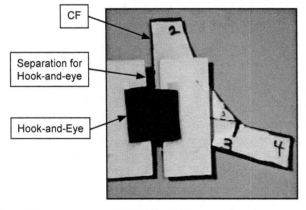

Step V. Create the Back Band Pattern

The Back Band pattern must be adjusted for the following factors:

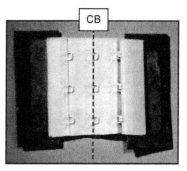

- The height and width of the back closure based on the number of hook-and-eye rows and columns.
- The size of the top and bottom band elastic.
- The selection of a T-Intersection or Integrated Strap.
- The amount of stretch determined from the inhale/exhale measurements on page 111.

1. Trace the shape of the Back Band design on a new sheet of paper.
2. Measure the height of the hook-and-eye tape and mark this on the back of the pattern. If necessary, adjust the height of the Back Band design.
3. Add a seam allowance to the top of the pattern that is equal to the width of the top band elastic.
4. Add a seam allowance to the bottom of the pattern that is equal to the width of the bottom band elastic plus 1/8" (3 mm).
5. If an Integrated Strap is used, adjust the shape of the last fourth of the pattern that is closest to Center Back.
6. As a final step in the fitting procedure, connect the hook-and-eye tape for the back closure, then shorten the Back Band by the width of the two tapes. This optimizes comfort by compensating for the stretch factor of the fabric used.

This Back Closure was cut from a length of hook-and-eye tape.

The height of the back opening is based on the number hook-and-eye rows.

The width is based on the number of eye columns. The Center Back should fall in the middle of the width.

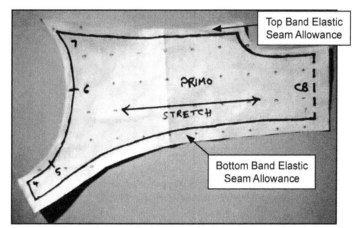

Back Band Pattern for "Y" Centerpiece Bra
(Integrated Strap)

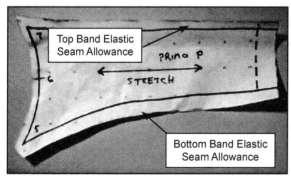

Back Band Pattern for Partial Band Bra
(T-Intersection Strap)

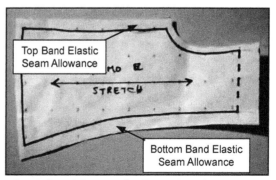

Back Band Pattern for Extended Centerpiece
(Integrated Strap)

VI. Back Band Breathing Allowance

For a bra to be comfortable, the wearer's breathing must not be constricted. So the Back Band must have an adequate stretch factor to compensate for the difference between the Rib Cage Inhale and Exhale measurements as established on page 111.

If the Back Band is made only of stretch fabric such as Powernet or Powerknit, or covered with a knit fabric such as Tricot, there should be adequate stretch. If the stretch fabric is covered with a woven fashion fabric, cutting the fabric on the bias might provide adequate stretch. If the amount of stretch is inadequate, create a second expanded Back Band pattern for the fashion fabric.

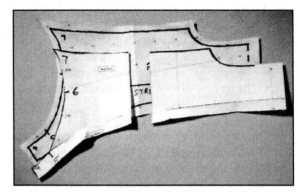

Breathing Allowance for Woven Fabric

1. To determine if the Back Band fabric will stretch an adequate amount, cut the original sloper design apart as shown in the photo.
2. Separate the two pieces by half the difference between the Inhale and Exhale Rib Cage measurements.
3. Verify the Back Band fabric will stretch from the smaller pattern size to the larger pattern size. For woven fashion fabric, stretch it on the true bias.
4. If the fashion fabric does not stretch an adequate amount, create a second expanded Back Band pattern.

VII. Sew a Trial Muslin Bra

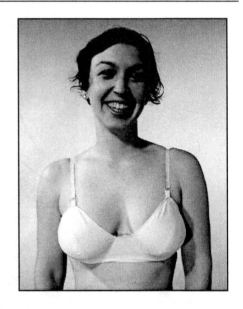

1. Cut out all the pattern pieces from muslin.
2. Sew the Bra Cup pieces, then press open.
3. If you are making a Full Band bra, sew the Centerpiece to the Back Band, then press open.
4. Sew the Bra Cups to the Centerpiece and Back Band, then press open.
5. Sew a line of stay stitching around the outside edges of the bra.
6. Press under the bra's outside edges to the stay stitching from Step 5, then topstitch in place.
7. Sew Velcro for a Center Back closure.
8. To test a bra for an underwire, topstitch underwire channeling just outside the Bra Cup seam, then insert the underwire.
9. If necessary, add bias tape for bra straps.
10. Verify the pattern's fit.
11. Record the length required for the Shoulder Strap in the Bra Specification sheet.

For an example of a completed Bra Specification Sheet for this bra, see page 129.

Sample Bra Specification Sheet

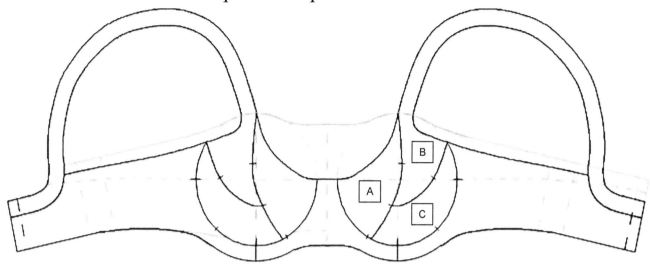

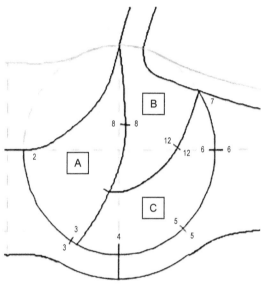

Date: _4/1/2017_

Bra Wearer: _Alex_

Sloper Name: _Basic (1/1/2017)_

Bra Name: _Primo_

Style: _Y center Full Band bra_

Type - Full Band: _X_   or Partial Band _____

Strap - Integrated: _X_   T-Intersection _____

Length: _15"_   Fabric: _____

Underwire - No: _____   Yes - Size: _38_

Rib Cage - Exhale: _27"_   Inhale: _30"_   Stretch: _2"_

Cup Fabric: _Silk Charmeuse_

Band Fabric: _Powernet_

Hook-and-Eye Rows: _3_   Height of Tape: _2"_

Eyes per Row (1-3): _3_   Decrease CB: _1/2"_

Construction Sequence:

1 _Bra Cup "B" + "C"_

2 _Bra Cup "A" + "BC"_

3 _Centerpiece + Back Band_

4 _Bra Cup "ABC" + Back Band/Centerpiece_

5 _Bottom Elastic_

6 _Channeling_

7 _Attach Straps to top of Bra Cup_

8 _Sew top band elastic_

9 _Attach straps to Back Band_

10 _Install underwires_

11 _Sew back closinG-Hook-and-eye tape_

Sewing the Bra

Bra Cups are sewn to minimize the bulk of the seam allowances and to provide maximum strength at critical points. The elastic must be sewn so that the stitching does not break while the bra is being worn.

Bra Cup Seams

Bra Cups are sewn using either plain seams with topstitching or fake flat-fell seams. The plain seam minimizes the bulk where one seam intersects with another. But the plain seam is totally dependent on the strength of the sewing thread to hold the fabric together. The flat-fell seam sews both seam allowances to one side of the fabric thus adding strength to the seam.

For knit fabric, the topstitching can be straight stitching as the fabric will not unravel with washing. But for woven fabric, zigzag the topstitching.

After the seams are sewn and topstitched, trim the seam allowance close to the stitching by holding your scissors at a slight angle while pressing the seam against the scissors with your other hand. Be careful not to cut the fabric or the thread from the topstitching.

Bra Band Stitches

Bra Band elastic must be sewn using a zigzag stitch. The initial line of stitching can be a small width. But the second line should be a three-step zigzag or serpentine stitch.

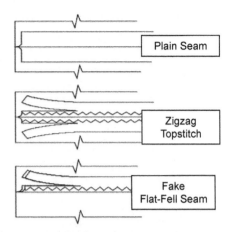

Plain Seam

Zigzag Topstitch

Fake Flat-Fell Seam

Trim the Seam Allowance Close to the Stitching

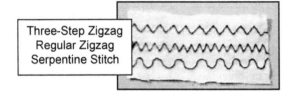

Three-Step Zigzag
Regular Zigzag
Serpentine Stitch

Step I. Sew the Bra Cup and Band

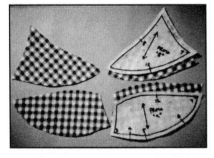

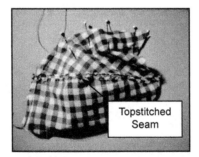

Topstitched Seam

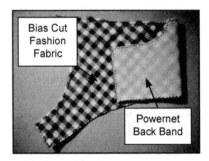

Bias Cut Fashion Fabric

Powernet Back Band

1. Using the patterns, cut the fabric for the bra.
2. Take two parts of the Bra Cup and arrange them so there is a left and right side.
3. Pin and sew the two parts together, then press open.

4. From the right side, topstitch the seam allowances following close to the seam.
5. Trim the excess seam allowance.
6. Repeat steps 2 to 5 until both Bra Cups are complete.

7. If a covering fabric is being used for the Back Band, zigzag it to the Powernet.
8. For a Full Band bra, sew the Centerpiece to the Back Band and topstitch, then sew the Bra Cups to the band with a plain seam.
9. If no underwire or channeling is going to be used, press both seam allowances away from the Bra Cup, then topstitch as a flat-fell seam.

Step II. Sew the Bottom Band Elastic

When creating a Full Band bra, sew the elastic to the full length of the bra. For a Partial Band bra, sew the elastic to the Back Band and Centerpiece.

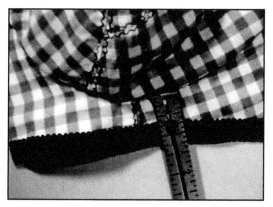 

1. Place the bra right side up.
2. Place the band elastic on the bra with the soft side up. The picot edge should be facing the body of the bra.
3. Hand baste the elastic to the bra band. The outside edge of the elastic should follow the outside of the seam allowance. Verify that the elastic's picot edge is spaced at least the width of the elastic from the Bra Cup seam plus 1/8" (3 mm).
4. Use a narrow zigzag to attach the picot edge to the bra. The stitching should be as close to the edge of the elastic as possible without going over the edge.
5. Remove the basting.
6. Trim the bottom seam allowance.

7. Turn the elastic to the inside of the bra.
8. Hand baste the elastic so the picot edge is exposed only along the bottom edge of the bra.
9. From the inside, sew a three-step zigzag or serpentine stitch to attach the elastic to the Bra Band. This line of stitching should follow the edge of the elastic that is opposite the small zigzag sewn in Step 4.
10. Remove the basting.
11. If you are creating a Partial Band bra, sew the Bra Cups to the Centerpiece and Back Bands, and then stay stitch around the bottom of the Bra Cup.

Note: Do not sew the elastic over the Bra Cup seam allowance as the underwire channeling will be sewn to this seam allowance.

Sew the Front closing to the Bra Cup Extension

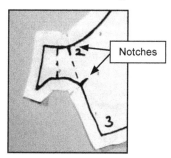 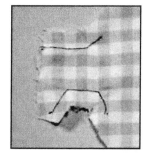 

If you are adding a front closing device, sew it now.

1. Add sewing notches to the top and bottom of where the front closing extension meets the underwire line.

2. Sew a line of stay stitching along the top and bottom of the front closing extension, extending the stay stitching 1/4" (6 mm) beyond the sewing notches, then clip.

3. Press under the seam allowances, then thread the extension through the front closing device.
4. Use a zipper foot to sew a line of stitches to attach the front closing device.

Step III. Sew the Underwire Channeling

Channeling is used to hold the underwire. Even empty, however, channeling adds extra support to a bra.

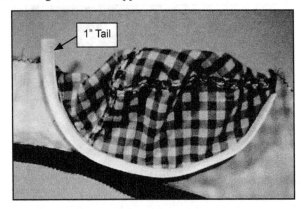

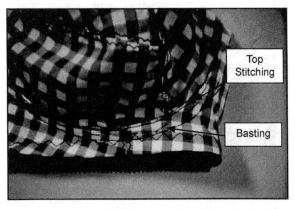

1. Turn the bra wrong side out and expose the seam allowance around the Bra Cup's bottom so channeling can be sewn just to this seam allowance.
2. Place the channeling on top of the seam allowance. If you are creating a Full Band Bra, place the channeling on top of the Bra Cup seam allowance. If you are creating a Partial Band Bra, place the channeling on top of the Back Band seam allowance. The channeling stitches should be closest to the Bra Cup and start 1/2" (13 mm) down from the underarm seam.
3. Sew the channeling to the seam allowance, matching the channel's edge to the underwire seam, stopping 1/2" (13 mm) from the top of the Centerpiece's raw edge.
4. Leave a 1" (2.5 cm) tail above the Centerpiece, then cut off the excess channeling.

5. Hand baste the channeling flat against the bra. For a Full Band bra, the channeling should be basted to the band. For a Partial Band bra, the channeling should be basted to the Bra Cup.
6. From the outside of the bra, topstitch the channeling to the bra close to the edge of the Bra Cup seam.
7. From the inside of the bra, topstitch the opposite edge of the channeling, keeping the two rows of stitching parallel to each other.
8. Remove the basting.

Note: When you topstitch the channeling, be careful the stitching catches the channeling just along the edges and does not close off the channel opening for the underwire.

Padded Straps

Use the pattern below to create a padded strap that is wider across the top of the shoulder than the Bra Strap by itself. Sew a 3/4" (2 cm) strap to each end to extend the length as required.

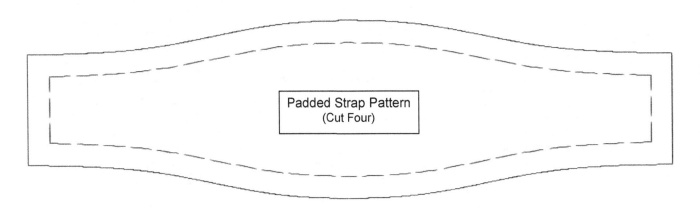

Step IV. Prepare the Straps

Straps can have a number of different configurations, as shown in the list to the right.

Straps can also be sewn on top of the band elastic or underneath. These instructions describe how to attach the straps underneath the elastic.

The first step in preparing straps is to attach the strap adjuster and ring.

1. Cut two short lengths of strap for the ring end. For integrated straps they need to be at least 2" (5 cm) longer than the curved edge of the Back Band. T-Intersection straps that extend to the bottom elastic need to be at least 2" (5 cm) longer than the height of the Back Band.
2. Cut two longer lengths for the slider end, each approximately the strap length recorded on the Bra Specification Sheet.
3. Loop the end of a short strap through a ring so that the non-shiny side touches, then sew. I recommend a combination of straight and zigzag stitching.
4. Loop the end of a long strap through a slider so that the non-shiny side touch, and then sew.
5. Repeat for the other straps.
6. Take the free end of a slider strap and thread it though a ring, then thread it through both sides of the slider so the shiny side is up, as illustrated.

Detachable Straps

Straps are made detachable with G-Hooks.

1. For detachable straps, cut two lengths of strap that are 2" (5 cm) longer than the strap length recorded on the Bra Specification Sheet.
2. Sew a slider on one end, then thread the other end of the strap through a G-Hook and back through the slider.
3. Sew a G-Hook on the other end of the strap.

Bra Strap Variations

- Integrated Strap
- T-Intersection Strap stopping at the top of the Back Band
- T-Intersection Strap stopping at the bottom of the Back Band
- Removable Straps
- Strap Tab on the Bra Cup
- Strap adjusters in front or back
- Straps that are stretch, no-stretch, or a combination.
- Padded Straps
- Fashion Fabric Straps

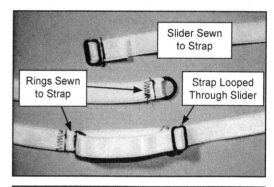

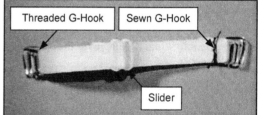

Detachable Strap

Step V. Attach the Straps

Straps can be attached in several ways. To attach straps under the top band elastic, follow these steps.

1. Place the strap shiny side down on the bra's good side with the end of the strap to be sewn matched to the seam allowance's top edge.
2. Sew one row of stitching on the seam line.
3. Sew a second line of stitching on the seam allowance about 1/8" (3 mm) from the seam line.

After the band elastic is sewn and turned, the strap will then be facing the correct direction for going over the shoulder.

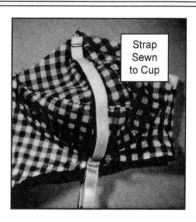

Step VI. Sew the Top Elastic

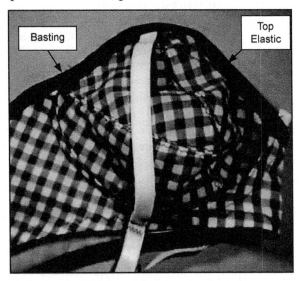

1. Place the bra right side up.
2. Place the band elastic on the bra with the soft side up. The picot edge should be facing the body of the bra.
3. Hand baste the elastic to the Bra Band and Cup. The outside edge of the elastic should follow the outside of the seam allowance. The elastic can be stretched slightly along the underarm area of the Bra Cup.
4. Use a narrow zigzag to attach the picot edge to the bra. The stitching should be as close to the edge of the elastic as possible without going over the edge.

5. Remove the basting.
6. Turn the elastic to the inside of the bra.
7. Hand baste the elastic so the picot edge is exposed only along the top edge of the bra.
8. Use a three-step zigzag or serpentine stitch to sew the elastic to the Bra Band. This line of stitching should follow the edge of the elastic that is opposite the zigzag sewn in Step 4.
9. Remove the basting.

Step VII. Sew the Integrated Strap

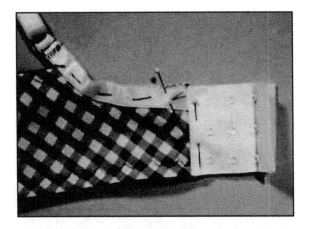

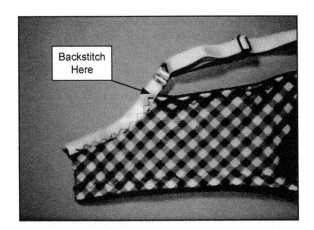

If you are using an Integrated Strap, sew it at this time.
1. Lay the ring end of the strap on top of the Back Band, shiny side up.
2. Verify that the strap is not twisted and hand baste.
3. Verify that the strap will reach the correct height of the back closure.

4. Remove the back closure and sew the strap to the Back Band using a three-step zigzag or serpentine stitch.
5. Back stitch carefully where the strap meets the top of the Back Band.
6. Remove the basting, then trim the seam allowance.

Step VIII. Add the Underwire

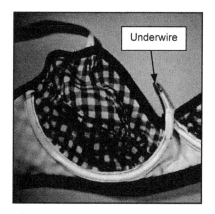

1. Sew across the channeling at the underarm location with several parallel rows of stitching.

2. Insert the underwire in the channeling through the Center Front opening. The Center Front end of an underwire usually is colored and shorter than the side.

3. Sew across the channeling at the Center Front location with several parallel rows of stitching.
4. Trim off the end of the channeling.

Step IX. Sew the Hook-and-Eye Tape

Before adding the hook-and-eye tape, verify the bra's fit. The Center Back opening should be adjusted according to the width of the hook-and-eye tape as described on page 127. This tape encloses the unfinished edge at back.

The width that the tape adds to the back of the bra depends on whether there is one, two, or three columns of eyes. The example shown below has three columns of eyes and adds an inch to the length of the bra's back.

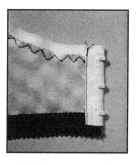

1. Fold back the top edge of the tape's eye side and place the left end of the bra's back close to the fold, then sew.

2. Fold the top edge back over the end of the bra band and stitch in place.
3. Zigzag the eye tape's outside edges.

4. Center the tape's hook side over the Bra Band's right end with the hooks facing up.
5. Sew the tape to the bra band.

6. Fold the hooks to the inside of the bra band and sew in place.
7. Zigzag the outside edges.

Bra Design Variations

Possible bra designs are unlimited. The previous chapter includes instructions for creating either a Full or Partial Band Bra. The instructions are for sewing an Integrated Strap to the Back Band. Sewing the strap to the top of the Back Band would turn it into a T-Intersection Strap.

This chapter shows how to test a Bra Cup design with chip or poster board, use a Cupless Bra, or use the mold making process to create a low back, strapless bra that cannot be made directly from a sloper.

The Bra Specification Sheet on page 141 is for recording designs. For additional design suggestions, see page 140.

Poster Board Bra Cup

Patterns for new designs for Bra Cups can be cut out of poster board and taped together. These poster board cups can be held up against a muslin sloper to verify fit. The example below shows this process along with the finished bra. Notice the finished bra is an example of a T-Intersection Strap in the back.

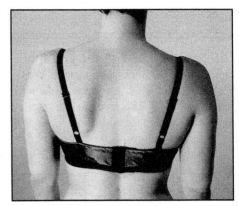

Poster Board Cup   Finished Bra   T-Intersection Strap

Bra Strap Position

Generally Bra Cups are best supported when the straps are attached at the top of the Apex line. Illustrated below is a Balconette Bra for which the straps are at the side of the body. It is always best to test extreme design variations with a muslin version.

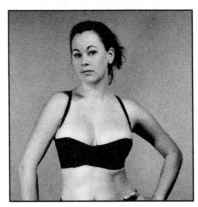

Muslin Test Bra   Finished Balconette Bra

Cupless Bra

The primary fitting elements of a bra are the Bra Cup and the Bra Band around the rib cage. If a bra requires adjustment in a fitting, the issue can be with the Bra Cup or the Bra Band or both. The best way to verify fit is to create a Cupless Bra which includes all the parts of a Full Band Bra less the Bra Cups.

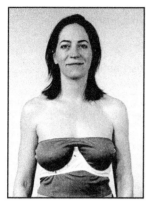
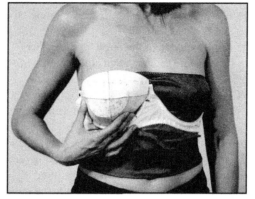

Cupless Bra   Cupless Bra with Poster Board Cup   Finished Bra

Push-Up Bra

The Push-Up Bra presents a particular challenge because it must cover both the breast and the push-up padding. In the example below, Velcro was cut to a 1/4" (6 mm) width and sewn to a Cupless Bra's underwire seam. The padding was then held in place with double-sided Velcro to make a Press'n Seal mold. After the mold was removed from the body, the inside of the Bra Cup was also treated with Press'n Seal to create a pocket for the push-up padding.

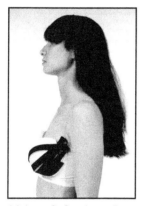
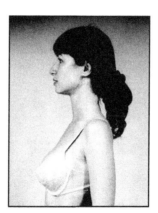

Velcro & Cupless Bra   Finished Bra

Bullet Bra

Prior to underwires, the 1950s Bullet Bra had straps sewn to the top of the Apex line. While many versions of the bullet bra used a combination of seams, one was shaped with a single dart. To make this style Bra Cup, follow these steps:

1. Measure the Full Bust line over the Bra Cup from underwire to underwire.
2. Use this measurement as the diameter to draw a circle on chip (or poster) board.
3. Cut a dart line from one edge of the circle to the center.
4. Place the chip board over the breast and adjust the size of the dart until the cup fits snugly.
5. Tape the Bra Cup closed and hold it up to a Cupless Bra.
6. To adjust the direction that the "bullet" points, trim the inside of the Bra Cup.

Note: Step 6 compensates for the breast tissue extending around the side of the body which causes the bullet's apex to point to the side. By trimming the Center Front of the Bra Cup, the apex can be adjusted for a straight ahead position.

In the example below, the Bullet Bra was shaped while the mold is being made.

Period Bullet Bra   Chip Board Bullet Bra Cup

 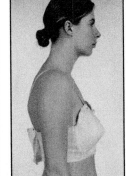 

Muslin Bullet Bra   Finished Bullet Bra

Low-Back Strapless Bra

A low-back strapless bra for a formal gown or wedding dress cannot be made directly from a bra sloper. Nor can support for this type of bra come from the rib cage directly below the breast. So, as illustrated below, support comes from a 2" (5 cm) elastic around the waist between the rib cage and the hip bone that is extended to the Bra Cups with boning.

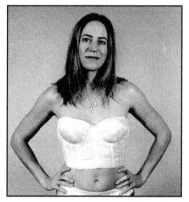 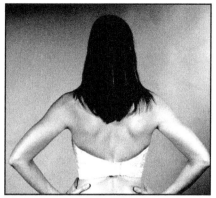 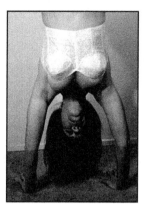

Strapless, Low-Back Bra   Testing the Fit

This bra was made by creating a mold for this specific design using the Press'n Seal technique. Boning was added at Center Front, under the Bust Apex, and at the side.

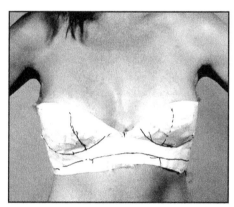 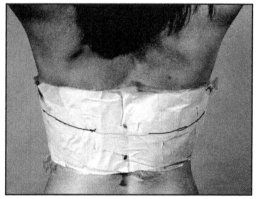

Press'n Seal Mold

Bra Design Examples

Below, on the left, are design configurations for diverse bra styles. Photocopy the images on the right for drawing original design ideas.

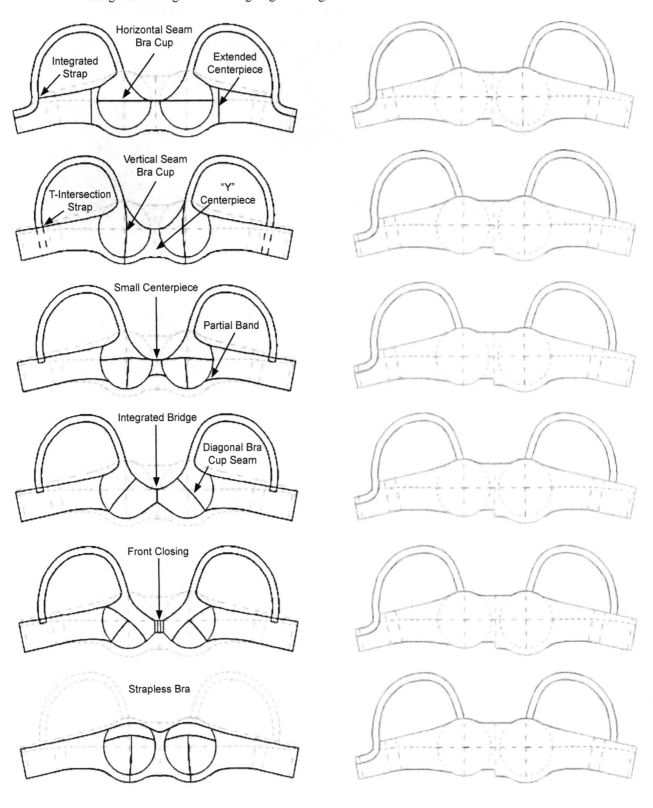

Horizontal Seam
Bra Cup

Integrated
Strap

Extended
Centerpiece

Vertical Seam
Bra Cup

T-Intersection
Strap

"Y"
Centerpiece

Small Centerpiece

Partial Band

Integrated Bridge

Diagonal Bra
Cup Seam

Front Closing

Strapless Bra

Bra Specification Sheet

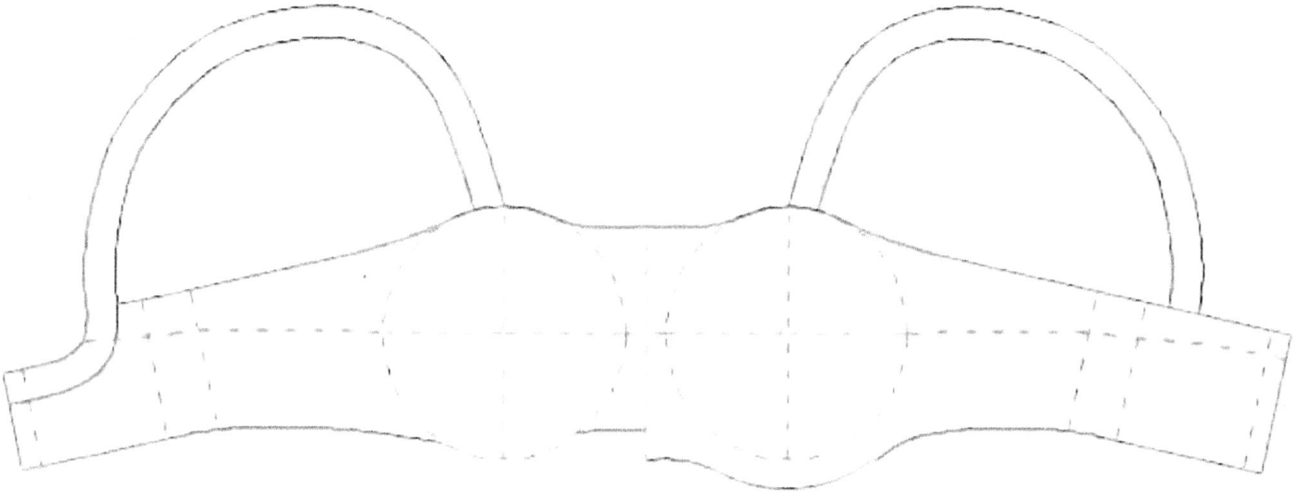

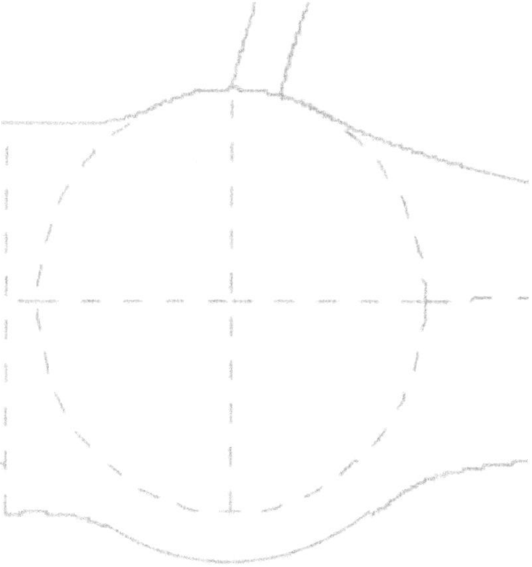

Date: _____

Bra Wearer: _____

Sloper Name: _____

Bra Name: _____

Style: _____

Type - Full Band: _____ or Partial Band _____

Strap - Integrated: _____ T-Intersection _____

Length: _____ Fabric: _____

Underwire - No: _____ Yes - Size: _____

Rib Cage - Exhale: _____ Inhale: _____ Stretch: _____

Cup Fabric: _____

Band Fabric: _____

Hook-and-eye Rows: _____ Height of Tape: _____

Eyes/Row (1-3): _____ Decrease CB: _____

Construction Sequence:

1 _____

2 _____

3 _____

4 _____

5 _____

6 _____

7 _____

8 _____

9 _____

10 _____

11 _____

Athletic Bras

Athletic Bras are designed specifically for knit fabrics which assume a three-dimensional shape without darts or shaping from seams. Only needing side and shoulder seams and some form of edge finish, they are relatively easy to make. The fit must be adjusted for the stretch of the specific fabric used. If a knit is very stretchy, it may be necessary to use a lining, such as Powernet, that can provide more tension.

Qty	Materials for Athletic Bras
1 box	Press'n Seal
1 roll	2" Masking Tape
1/2 yd	Fashion Fabric
2 yds	1/4" (6 mm) Elastic for edging
1 yd	1" (25 mm) Elastic for Rib Cage
1/2 yd	Powernet (optional)
1/2 yd	Knit Lining Material (optional)
2 yds	Fold Over Elastic (optional)

 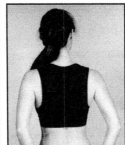 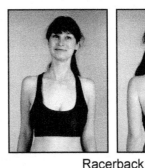 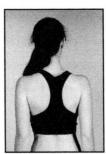

Full Back   Racerback

 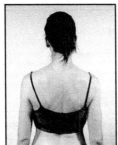  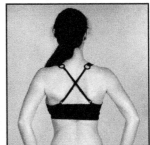

Fabric Straps   Decorative Straps

The Design Process

To make an Athletic Bra pattern, first create a master pattern from a mold that compresses the breast tissue from just above the breast down to the rib cage. This master pattern can then be used to create patterns for individual designs. Finally, these patterns must be cut from knit and given a trial fitting to adjust for the fabric's stretch. Listed below are the steps for this procedure:

1. Create a mold that compresses the body.
2. Mark design lines on the bra mold.
3. Convert the mold to a master pattern paper.
4. Use the master pattern to create patterns for a specific design.
5. Cut the fabric from the design pattern, then baste for a fitting.
6. Correct the paper pattern, then finish the bra.

Note: When creating a pattern for an Athletic Bra, verify that the fabric and elastic will stretch enough to be pulled over the head.

Pull Over Measurement

_____

Creating an Athletic Bra Mold Using Press'n Seal

To create a mold for an Athletic Bra, the goal is to compress the breast tissue to reduce unwanted movement even during strenuous exercise.

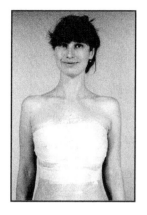 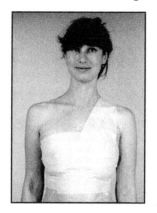 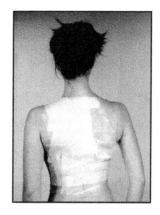 

1. Wrap Press'n Seal around the entire body from above the bust to the rib cage, compressing breast tissue.
2. After the body is completely covered with Press'n Seal, apply masking tape.

3. Wrap Press'n Seal over the shoulder and down the back, then cover with masking tape.

4. On the back, make sure the masking tape covers the body where you intend to add design lines.

5. You may opt to use an existing Athletic Bra to trace design lines onto the masking tape. Just draw in the line desired on one side of the body.

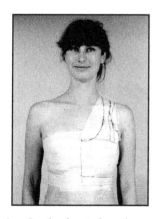 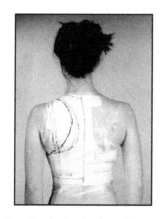 

6. On the front, draw in the design lines desired, including a Center Front and the location of the rib cage just below the breast tissue.

7. On the back, draw in the desired design lines, including a Center Back and the location of the rib cage just below the breast tissue.

8. To determine the best location for the shoulder seam, place a book or other flat object on top of the shoulder, then draw in the seam line.

Using the Mold for a Master Pattern

Since every knit has a different degree of stretch, the initial master pattern for an Athletic Bra is merely a guideline for an individual design.

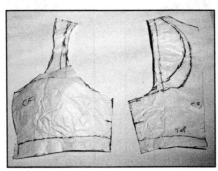

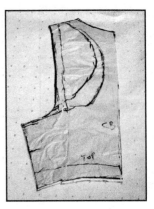

1. Remove the mold, then reinforce the inside with masking tape.

2. From the good side, cut the mold along the design lines. If you have multiple design lines for the upper torso, cut along the outside design lines.

3. Add sewing notches at the side and shoulder seams, then separate the front and back patterns along these lines.

4. Place the back mold on a piece of pattern paper, then trace the shape. The back pattern may lay fairly flat.

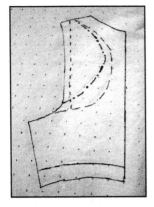

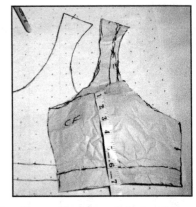

5. Place the pattern paper for the back on top of the mold and trace any alternate design lines you have made.

6. Place the front mold onto a piece of pattern paper, then trace the front mold's outline. Due to the contours of the body, this mold may not lay flat.

7. To transfer internal design lines from the mold, measure from the edge of the mold to the design lines, then use these measurements to complete the master pattern.

Creating an Athletic Bra Design

To create a new design for an Athletic Bra, follow these steps:
1. Trace the design lines desired from the master pattern to new pattern paper.
2. Add a 1" (25 mm) elastic allowance at the rib cage.
3. Add 1/2" (12 mm) seam allowances to the side and shoulder seams.
4. Add 1/4" (6 mm) seam allowances to the neck and armhole seams.
5. Use the patterns to cut the knit fashion fabric.
6. If the fashion fabric is to be reinforced with powernet, use the same patterns to cut the powernet, then zigzag the powernet to the fashion fabric.
7. Machine baste the side and shoulder seams for a trial fitting.

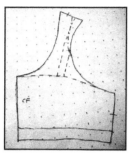     

Master Pattern   The Racerback Athletic Bra

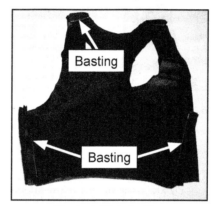

Basted Athletic Bra

Fitting an Athletic Bra

The Athletic Bra must be adjusted for the fabric used.
1. Put the basted bra on the wearer, wrong side out.
2. Pin the side seams for the fit desired.
3. Remove the bra, then baste the new side seams for a second fitting.
4. Put the basted bra on again. Then, to establish the length of the rib cage elastic, pin it on the body for the tension desired.
5. Remove the bra. Then, based on the fitting, adjust the patterns.

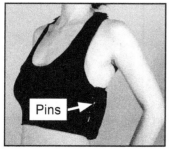   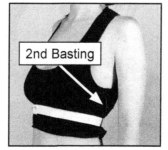

Pinned Bra   Rib Cage Elastic

Elastic for Rib Cage

Sewing Athletic Bras

Athletic Bras are relatively easy to sew. The main styling choice is how to finish the neckline and armhole edges. This can be done by encasing non-decorative elastic inside the bra, using fold over elastic, or using fashion fabric for the edging. The elastic at the rib cage is most often encased inside the bra.

Encasing Non-Decorative Elastic Inside Bra

Once the pattern for a specific design has had a trial fitting, the Athletic Bra can be completed by finishing the edges with non-decorative elastic encased inside the bra, see page 18. This is a common finish for rib cage elastic. For this example, a cotton T-shirt knit was added as an underlining to the bra's front for additional body and to minimize show through.

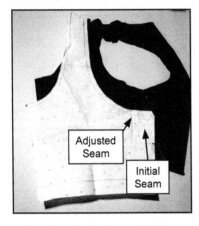
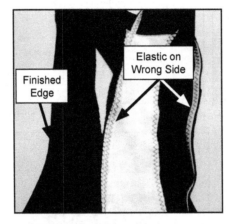

1. Based on the fitting, adjust the patterns.
2. Remove the basting, then use the adjusted patterns to trim the fabric.
3. Pin, then sew the shoulder and side seams using a 1 mm zigzag stitch.
4. Press open the sewn seams, then use a 2 mm to topstitch the seam allowances in place.
5. Trim off the excess seam allowance.

6. Pin 1/4" (6 mm) elastic around the armhole and neckline on the wrong side of the fabric close to the edge of the fashion fabric.
7. Use a 3 mm zigzag stitch to sew the elastic to the bra down the middle of the elastic.
8. Turn the elastic to the inside of the fabric and zigzag in place.
9. Cut the rib cage elastic to the length established on page 145 plus 1" (2.5 cm).
10. Pin the rib cage elastic in a loop with a 1" (2.5 cm) overlap.

11. Use a 1 mm long, 4 mm wide zigzag stitch to sew the elastic closed.
12. Pin the elastic to the wrong side of the bra's bottom edge.
13. Use a 2 mm wide zigzag stitch to sew the elastic's bottom edge to the bra, stretching as necessary.
14. Use a zigzag stitch to sew the top of the elastic to the bra.
15. Turn the elastic to the inside of the bra, then sew a 4 mm or decorative zigzag along the top edge of the elastic.

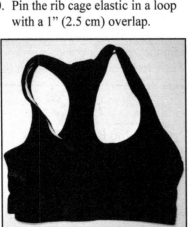

Finished Athletic Bra

Sewing Fold Over Elastic

Fold over elastic can be used as the finish for an Athletic Bra's neckline and armholes. Fold over elastic has a groove down the center. The finished edge of a garment is aligned with this groove, placing half the fold over on the wrong side of the garment, half on the good side.

For this example of the Athletic Bra, a cotton compression Lycra is added as an underlining to reinforce the stretch factor of the knit fashion fabric.

1. Sew the side and shoulder seams.
2. Trim any seam allowance from the neck and armhole seams.
3. From the good side of the fashion fabric, hand baste the edge of the bra to the groove of the foldover elastic, wrong side to wrong side.
4. Use a 3 mm zigzag to sew the elastic to the bra.
5. Wrap the fold over elastic to the good side of the fashion fabric, then zigzag in place. This can be done with a decorative zigzag stitch such as the three-step or serpentine stitch, see page 130.
6. Finish the bottom of the bra as described on page 146.

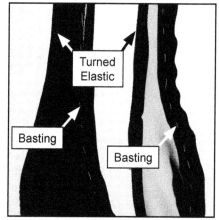

Fold Over Elastic

Sewing Fashion Fabric Straps

Once a design's pattern has had a trial fitting, an Athletic Bra with fashion fabric straps can be made by following these steps:

1. Measure the front and back neck openings, then cut fashion fabric strips those lengths by 1-1/2" (38 mm) wide. The direction of maximum stretch should follow the length of the strap.
2. Measure the length needed for the shoulder straps from the front side seam to the back side seam. Use the master pattern to determine the length needed for over the shoulder. Cut fashion fabric strips that length by 1-1/2" (38 mm) wide. The direction of maximum stretch should follow the length of the strap.
3. Cut 1/4" (6 mm) elastic to the lengths determined in steps 1 and 2.
4. Zigzag the elastic along the all the fashion fabric straps' edges.
5. On the bra's body, trim any seam allowance from the neck and armhole seams.
6. Pin the strap for the front neckline so the elastic's edge matches the edge of the garment's body, good side to good side, then zigzag in place.
7. Wrap the strap to the inside of the body and hand baste in place to ensure a smooth "corded" finish to the neckline. Then, from the good side, use a 1 mm zigzag to secure the strap to the garment's body.
8. Trim off the excess strap allowance.
9. For the back neckline, repeat steps 6 through 8.
10. For the shoulder straps, follow steps 6 through 8 to sew the straps to the front armhole, starting at the side seam.
11. Use a fitting to establish the correct length of the shoulder strap, pinning it to the back armhole, then follow steps 6 through 8 to secure the shoulder strap to the back armhole, ending at the side seam.
12. Wrap the strap's fashion fabric around the elastic and zigzag it in place.

Bra with Straps

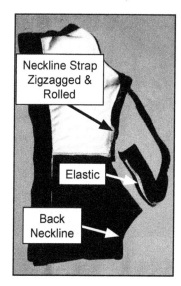

Designing a Wedding Dress

Designing an original garment may seem overwhelming. But breaking down a design into a series of steps that determine specific aspects makes the process very manageable. And creating a wedding dress can be a good choice for a beginning designer since the aspects influencing design decisions are clear: the occasion; the time of day the garment will be worn; and the person wearing it. Furthermore, there is probably a commitment to take the time to create the best possible dress.

There is also a lot of guidance available for decisions specific to a wedding dress. Doing some research and looking at what others have created allows for replicating a look or combining elements from different designs to create something fresh. Choice of fabric is of paramount importance and needs to be made early in the design process. In Western cultures, white has long been a standard color choice, but there is no reason it has to be. Fabric content is a critical consideration as well.

The following section illustrates the process for making specific design decisions and offers suggestions for possible variations. For the top, the Bust Sling Bra pattern is used and several styling choices for the front and the back are provided. The waistline of the skirt starts at the rib cage just below the bust and either closely follows the body or has some fullness. The two examples provided are: an A-Line skirt with a custom made Hoop Petticoat; a Trumpet style skirt using a commercially available wedding petticoat.

A-Line Wedding Dress   Trumpet Wedding Dress

Design Choices

Select a Bust Sling variation for the top and determine the skirt's hem length.

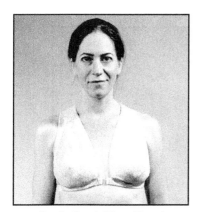

Basic Bust Sling Front

Princess Seam

Multi-Panel Front

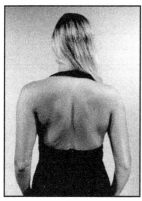

Halter Neck

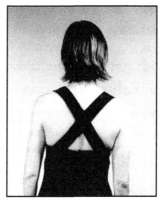

"X" Back

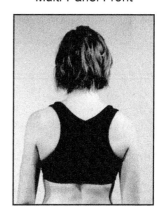

Racerback

Short Hem

Floor Length

Hoop Skirts

A hoop petticoat can be used to change a silhouette. This petticoat can either be custom made or purchased commercially.

Note: These petticoats hang from the waist because hanging from the rib cage would result in the petticoat either slipping down or placing too much weight on the shoulders.

| A-Line | Trumpet | A-Line with Train | Ball Gown |

Fabric Selection

Most wedding dresses use a combination of fabrics.

- **Brocade** - Fabric with raised, interwoven designs that does not drape as freely as lighter weight fabrics.
- **Charmeuse** - A lustrous, lightweight silk fabric that clings to curves.
- **Chiffon** - This sheer, lightly woven fabric drapes beautifully but needs an underlayer of fabric that is less transparent.
- **Crepe** - This lightweight fabric has a grainy, pebbled texture that drapes well but clings to the body.
- **Damask** - Fabric that has the appearance of brocade but is a lighter weight.
- **Dupioni** - A popular silk blend that has a coarser texture, comes in a variety of colors, and is less expensive than other silks.
- **Net** - A stiff, open weave fabric used to add shaping in petticoats.

- **Organza** - A slightly transparent fabric that is stiffer than chiffon. It is used for full skirts and overlays.
- **Satin** - This fabric has a sheen and comes in a variety of fiber content. The sheen of most satins comes from fibers that float over the top of the fabric. This can make it tricky to sew. The A-Line wedding dress in this book is made from a "Satin" Lycra that is an absolute joy to sew.
- **Taffeta** - A noisy fabric that wrinkles easily.
- **Tulle (Illusion)** - A very gauzy, lightweight fabric frequently used in wedding veils. Tulle is usually 54" in width, Illusion is twice the width.
- **Velvet** - A heavyweight fabric that has a distinctive directional texture. When you run your hand over it one way, it is smooth; in the opposite direction it is slightly rough. Maintain the same direction for adjoining panels in a dress or it will appear as if there are two different fabrics.

Bridal Lace

There are two basic types of bridal lace: trim in various widths and allover lace. Each comes in a wide variety of styles with repeat patterns that can be large or small. The patterns can be directional, with a distinct top and bottom, or not. Bridal Laces include:

- Knit Lace: Lacking a tulle back, this soft lace is flexible so contours around the body with ease.
- Venetian Lace: A firm, stiff lace without a net background on which patterns are created by close embroidered stitches.
- Embroidered Lace: Delicate patterns are tightly stitched onto a tulle base, forming the appearance of an applique.
- Chantilly Lace: Known for its abundant detail.
- Brocade: A class of richly decorative, shuttle-woven fabrics, often made in colored silks.
- Alençon: This needlepoint lace is usually found with a floral design on a sheer or net background.
- Eyelet Lace: A lightweight fabric pierced by small holes.

The laces in the two wedding dresses described here were chosen because their small, non-directional patterns simplified the construction process. When a lace's design is larger or directional, matching the lace to the shapes of the wedding dress' patterns can be challenging. For more distinct lace patterns, see the sewing instructions in Susan Khalye's *Bridal Couture* which shows how to overlap the lace.

Be Careful of Large Directional Patterns   Versatile Lace Pattern

Fabric Drape

The appearance of a garment can change dramatically based on how well a fabric drapes. A design that looks great in one fabric may appear stiff and inappropriate in another. The photos below show the drape of four different fabrics. These photos use a quarter scale Mini-Me Dress Form from waist to floor. The fabric is cut as a full circular skirt to show fullness with a train added.

Note: With softer fabrics, such as the silk, the train falls closer to the body while the polyester satin appears stiffer, hanging away from the body. The drape of the fabric at the side of the body also varies with Satin Lycra providing a clearly defined drape.

Instructions for making the Mini-Me Dress Form are included in the Appendix on page 167.

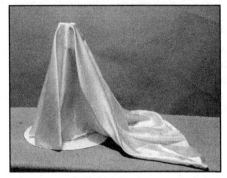
Silk Charmeuse

Rayon Satin

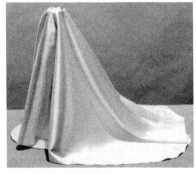
Satin Lycra

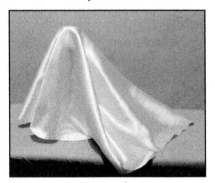
Polyester Satin

Train Length

The length of a train can vary considerably. The chart below shows the names that commonly identify the different lengths. One way to get an idea of what a train will look like is to try it in quarter scale (see chart below and page 172). Testing fabric on this scale before committing to a full size garment is strongly recommended.

Name	Full Size	CB Quarter Scale
Brush or Sweep	Just touching floor	11" (2.5 cm)
Court	One foot (30 cm)	13" (33 cm)
Chapel	Five feet (1.1 to 1.5 metres)	15" (38 cm)
Cathedral or Monarch	Eight feet (2.4 metres)	24" (61 cm)
Royal Cathedral	Ten feet (3 metres)	30" (76 cm)

Creating a Hoop Petticoat

A Hoop Petticoat is a reliable way to create a specific silhouette for a wedding dress. The dimensions of the petticoat are best determined in quarter scale first. The example here is for an A-Line Petticoat with seams at Side Front, Side Back, and Center Back. The hoops for this quarter scale can be plastic or cane boning or plastic cable ties. Shoe laces make convenient cording.

The Mini-Me Dress Form, described on page 167, has a circular base that is the size of the largest hoop which can pass through a standard 36" (90 cm) doorway without being manipulated.

Quarter Scale Hoop Petticoat

Qty	Materials
1	Dress Form, page 167
2 pair	Cording
1 roll	3/4" Masking Tape
1 yd	Hoop Boning
1 yd	Boning Casing
1/2 yd	Muslin
1 yd	Elastic, 3/4" or 5/8"
1/2 yd	Plastic Tube, page 155

1. Create a hoop that is the dimension of the circular floor pattern, then tape it closed.
2. Attach cords to the Waist Cross Section at Center Front, Center Back, and the two side seams.
3. Loop the cording around the hoop, lifting the hoop slightly off the floor, then tape in place.

4. Add hoops to establish the shape of the petticoat, taping each in place.

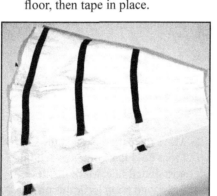

1/4 Scale Petticoat

5. Use different color cords to establish the locations of the Side Front and Side Back seams.
6. To create paper pattern(s) of the petticoat, measure the waist to floor dimension and location of the seams. To curve the hem and waist, see page 154.

7. Use the pattern(s) to cut muslin for a trial petticoat.
8. Sew the Side Front and Side Back seams.
9. Sew the casing at each hoop location.
10. Sew the Center Back seam.
11. Insert the boning into the casing.

Curving Hems and Waistlines

Full skirts, including Hoop Petticoats, require curved hems and waistlines. These instructions show how to curve the hem and waistline for a Hoop Petticoat as well as the location of each hoop. This technique can be used to create smooth curves for any full skirt. The following example creates a pattern for the front panel of the Hoop Petticoat.

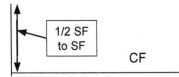
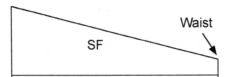
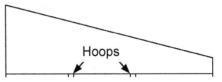

1. On the Mini-Me Dress Form, measure the distance from the waist to the floor, then draw a horizontal line this length. This is the Center Front fold line.

2. On the Mini-Me Dress Form, measure the distance between the two Side Front seams at the floor. Then, on the left end of the Center Front line, draw a vertical line that is half this length.

3. On the Mini-Me Dress Form, measure the distance between the two Side Front seams at the waist. Then, on the right end of the Center Front line, draw a vertical line that is half this length.

4. Draw a line to connect the top of the floor line with the top of the waist line. This is the Side Front seam.

5. Measure the distance from the waist to the hoops, then mark these locations on the Center Front line.

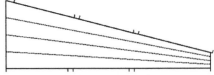

6. Fold the paper pattern along the Center Front line.

7. Fold the paper so the Center Front line coincides with the Side Front seam. Crease this fold.

8. Keeping the paper folded, mark the floor, waist, and hoop locations from the Center Front Fold onto the Side Front line.

9. Without opening the folded paper, fold it a second time so that the crease coincides with the Side Front line. Crease the new fold.

10. Unfold the pattern. There should now be three creases dividing the skirt equally into fourths. Mark these creases with dotted lines.

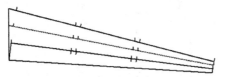
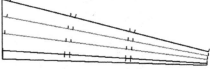

11. Fold the pattern so the Center Front Fold line is on the top dotted line. Mark the floor, waist, and hoop locations on this dotted line.

12. Move the pattern so that the Center Front Fold line coincides with the next dotted line. Mark the floor, waist, and hoop locations on this dotted line.

13. Move the pattern so that the Center Front Fold line coincides with the next dotted line. Mark the floor, waist, and hoop locations on this dotted line.

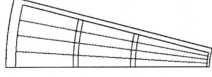

14. Unfold the pattern and connect the points on the dotted lines, then add seam allowances

Creating a Full Size Hoop Petticoat

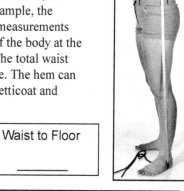

After the quarter scale Hoop Skirt has been created, the patterns can be enlarged to full size. For this example, the A-Line petticoat is a regular shape so the only measurements required for the pattern are the circumference of the body at the waist and the distance from the waist to floor. The total waist measurement should include 1" (2.5 cm) of ease. The hem can be determined by measuring the quarter scale petticoat and multiplying the result by 4.

Waist Circumference	Waist to Floor
_____	_____

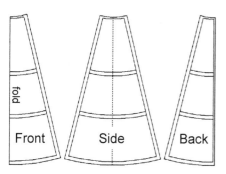

Front   Side   Back

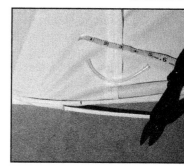

1. Create the patterns as described for the quarter scale hoop skirt. Add 1/2" (12 mm) seam allowances to the waist and center back. Add 1" (25 mm) seam allowances to the side seams and hem.
2. Use the patterns to cut the fabric.

3. Sew the Side Front and Side Back seams.
4. Sew the boning casing to the fabric, leaving a 2" (5 cm) opening each side of the Center Back seam.
5. Sew the Center Back seam, leaving an opening 12" (30 cm) from the waist down.

6. Insert the hoop boning into the top casing, allowing 4" (10 cm) of overlap.
7. Cut 6" of plastic tubing.

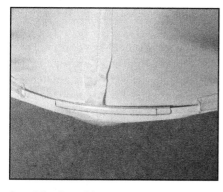

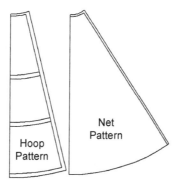

Hoop Pattern   Net Pattern

Finished Petticoat

8. Slip the tubing over one end of the boning, then insert the other end in the tubing to encase the boning's ends.

9. To soften the appearance of the hoops, cut a net skirt that uses the same waist measurement but is twice the width of the hem.
10. Finish the petticoat's top with a 1-1/2" (4 cm) wide waistband and hook and eye.

Creating an A-Line Wedding Dress

In this example, the Princess Style Bust Sling, page 78, has a Halter Back and a 1-1/2" (4 cm) wide Rib Cage Band. To support the skirt in back, straps are added between the halter at Center Back, passing diagonally down to the Rib Cage Band. The A-Line Skirt's front and side panels are Satin Lycra overlaid with lace. The back panel is Satin Lycra with double box pleats at the Rib Cage Band and a court length train. A Center Back zipper is the closing device with hook and eyes on the Rib Cage Band.

The patterns for the front and side panels of the skirt and a lining for the back are made using the same instructions as for the hoop skirt but different measurements.

I. Patterns for the Princess Seam Top

- The Halter Neck's Center Back (CB) can either be a fold or a seam that allows for fitting adjustments.
- The three-piece Prince Seam Top has sewing notches to verify the pieces are assembled correctly.
- All seam allowances for the top are 1/4" (6 mm).
- The Rib Cage Band is 1-1/2" (40 cm) in height. The length is the Inhale Rib Cage measurement plus a 1-1/2" (40 cm) overlap for a hook and eye closure.

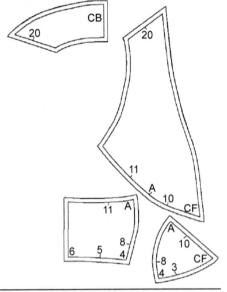

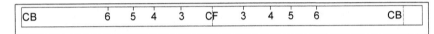

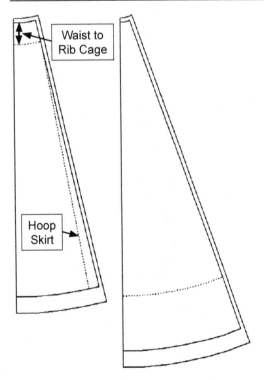

II. Patterns for the Skirt

This wedding dress is designed to have an overlay of lace on the front and side panels. Just a minimal amount of fullness is added to the circumference of the hem. To add pleats, see page 157

The front and side sections of an A-Line skirt are the same shape. For this design, a width of 8" (20 cm) is used for the front and back patterns' rib cage. The width of the Side Panel is adjusted for the body's circumference at the rib cage. Both patterns shown here are designed to be cut on the fold.

1. Lengthen the skirt by the distance between the rib cage and the waist.
2. To prevent the skirt from clinging too closely to the hoop petticoat, increase the hem by 2" (5 cm).
3. The back pattern includes a 1/2" (12 mm) seam at Center Back to allow for a zipper.
4. Add 3/4" (cm) to the waist and side seams and a 3" (cm) hem allowance.

III. Pleated Back Pattern

This example uses a Back Panel with a Restoration Period double box pleat on both sides of Center Back at the Rib Cage band.

> **Note:** This would be an ambitious project for a beginning sewer. The alternative would be to use the lining pattern for the fashion fabric and skip the pleating described in steps III and VI.

1. Start with the Back Panel that is not pleated. This pattern can be used for a lining.
2. To achieve the pleating desired, fold a separate piece of paper.
3. Carefully indicate the outside folds, shown as solid lines, and the inside folds, shown as dotted lines.
4. Place the pleated paper on top of the lining pattern and extend the waist and side seams to the width determined in Steps 2 and 3.

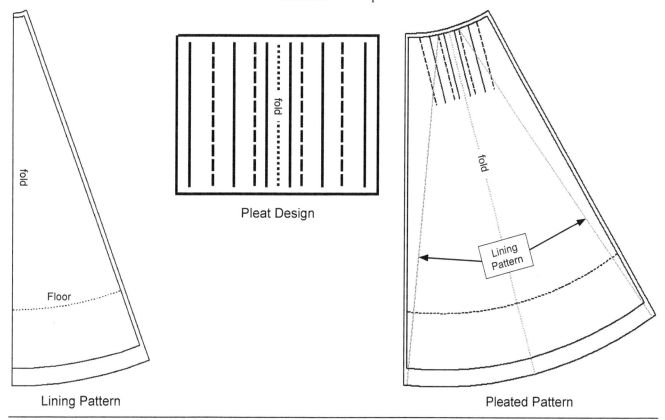

Lining Pattern

Pleat Design

Pleated Pattern

IV. Prepare for a Fitting

Lace is used as an overlay for the Bust Sling Top and the front and side panels of the skirt. It is not used for the Rib Cage Band. The lace at the bottom of the hem is positioned to take advantage of the lace's pattern, allowing the Satin Lycra to show through at the hem.

1. Cut the Bust Sling Patterns and the front and side Skirt Panels from the Satin Lycra and the lace overlay.
2. Zigzag the lace to the Satin.
3. Sew the Bust Sling Tops as described on page 91.
4. Sew the front Skirt Panel to the Side Panel.
5. Zigzag an Underlining to the Rib Cage Band.
6. Sew the Bust Sling Tops, then the Skirt Panels to the Rib Cage Band as described on page 91.

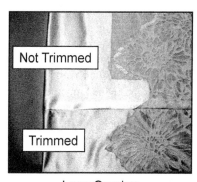

Lace Overlay

V. The Initial Fitting

This wedding dress is being made from Bust Sling Patterns that have already been fitted and the A-Line Hoop Petticoat shape. The panels are sewn for the front and side before the back panel with the train is added, so the only fitting that needs to be done at this point is to establish the length of the hem.

To determine the hem length, the Rib Cage Band should be parallel to the floor. This can be achieved by adding twill tape from the Center Back of the Halter Top down to the Rib Cage Band.

Front and Side Panels over Hoop Petticoat

VI. Pleat the Back Panel

These instructions show how to pleat the two sides of the Back Panel into an 8" (20 cm) finished width at the Rib Cage. If you are new to sewing, try it first on scrap fabric. When sewing the pleats, use a 4 mm stitch length starting at the waist. Do not back stitch at the bottom. This allows the length of the pleat stitching to be adjusted in order to optimize the appearance of the pleats in the finished garment.

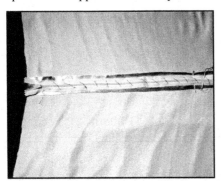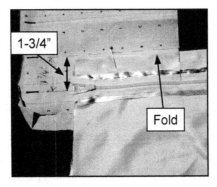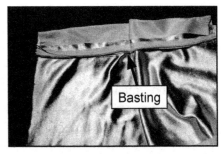

1. Sew the two panels together along the Center Back seam. The top of this seam should be a 6 mm basting stitch 12" (30 cm) long.
2. Hand baste the zipper to the top of the Center Back seam. Then, with a zipper foot, sew the zipper to the Center Back seam.
3. Remove the basting.

4. To start the Center Back side of the box pleats, pin one side of the Back Panel, good side to good side, so there is a fold 1-3/4" (44 mm) from the zipper teeth at Center Back.
5. Hand baste in place, then use the zipper foot to sew the first pleat along the same line of stitching used to sew the zipper.
6. Repeat Steps 4 and 5 for the other side.

7. To control the placement of the pleats' Center Back fold, hand baste the left to the right Back Panels next to the teeth edge of the zipper.

VI. Pleat the Back Panel (cont'd)

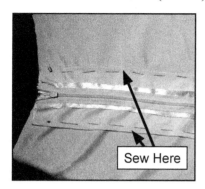

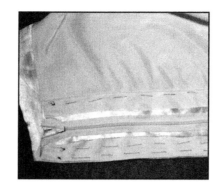

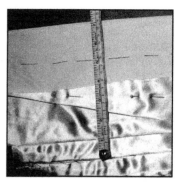

8. Open the back panel, then hand baste the pleats to the body of the skirt.
9. Sew a line of running stitches along the edge of the pleat. Stop at the bottom of the zipper.

10. Fold one side of the back panel along the edge of the first pleat, good side to good side, then hand baste 2" (5 cm) in from this edge.
11. Sew a line of running stitches 1" (2.5 cm) in from the edge, stopping at the bottom of the zipper.
12. Repeat Steps 10 and 11 for the other side.

13. To start a box pleat's outside fold, pin one side of the Back Panel so the fold is 7-1/4" (cm) from Center Back, then baste in place for the length of the zipper.

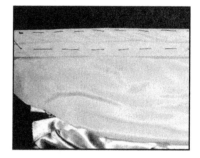

14. Use a Marks B Gone pen to draw a line that is 1-3/4" (4.4 cm) from the fold, then sew along this line, stopping at the bottom of the zipper. This creates the first outside pleat.

15. Open the back panel, then hand baste the pleat to the body of the skirt.
16. Sew a line of running stitches along the edge of the pleat. Stop at the bottom of the zipper.

17. Fold one side of the back panel along the edge of the first pleat, good side to good side, then hand baste 2" (5 cm) in from this edge.
18. Sew a line of running stitches 1" (2.5 cm) in from the edge, stopping at the bottom of the zipper.

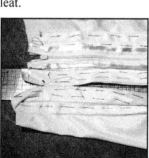

19. Whip stitch the inside folds of the box pleat together. Use a plastic ruler to avoid penetrating the pleat's face.
20. For the Back Panel's other side, repeat Steps 13 through 19.

VII. Complete the Dress

1. Hem the front and side panels.
2. Pin, then sew the back panel to the side panels.
3. Sew the back panel to the Rib Cage Band.
4. Cut a length of elastic for the Rib Cage Band, see page 92. The elastic should be the Elastic for Rib Cage measurement plus 1-1/2" (38 cm) for the hook-and-eye overlap.
5. Sew the elastic to both ends of the Rib Cage Band using a 2 mm wide zigzag stitch.
6. Add a lining to the inside of the Rib Cage Band, see Steps 11 to 13 on page 91.
7. Hem the train.
8. To soften the look of the hem, add a net ruffle to the bottom of the Hoop Petticoat that is twice the hoop's hem length.
9. Add straps from the Halter at Center Back to the Rib Cage Band.

Ruffle for Hoop Petticoat

Optional Beaded Straps

This example uses beaded straps. To make straps, the only technique you need to know is how to secure beading wire with a crimp tube and how to use a stop bead. The materials for the straps shown are listed below. They make a 12" (30 cm) long strap.

The length for the straps can be estimated during the initial fitting, page 158. The exact length should be determined during a final fitting before the bottom of the strap is permanently crimped. Once you have initially beaded the straps, sew them to the dress as follows:

1. Sew the top spacer bar to the Halter at Center Back.
2. To allow for fitting adjustment, sew a waistband loop to the Rib Cage Band. In this example, the strap is attached at the top of the skirt's side back seam.
3. Temporarily secure the bottom of the strap to the waistband loop.
4. Have the wearer try the wedding dress on and adjust the strap length to keep the Rib Cage Band parallel to the floor. To establish the correct length, add or remove beading as necessary.
5. Remove the dress and secure the length of the straps with crimp beads.

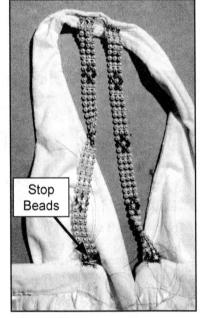

Stop Beads

Straps for Fitting

Beaded Straps

Qty	Materials
200	Swarovski Pearls: white, round, 6 mm
36	Swarovski Bicone Crystals: black diamond ab, 6 mm
1 hank	Czech Glass Rondelles: metallic brown iris, 11/0
24	Spacer Bars: silver-plated brass, 3 strand, 17 x 4 mm
1 roll	Fine Beading Wire: .014" diameter
12	Crimp Beads
6	Stop Beads

Creating a Trumpet Style Wedding Dress

The trumpet style wedding dress shown here is very quick and easy to make. The material is knit fabric with a subtle brocade-like pattern, and the wedding petticoat for a trumpet style skirt is commercially available. The knit allows the dress to be a pull over requiring no separate closing device.

This example uses a three-piece Princess Seam Bust Sling pattern with a halter neck. The skirt is styled from simple measurements for a front and back pattern with side seams. The skirt's top is finished with plush elastic. There is a horizontal seam on the skirt joining the fitted top to the Flared bottom.

I. Take the Measurements

1. To establish the position of the Center Front, Side and Center Back locations, tie 60" (150 cm) shoe laces to the Rib Cage Band of a trial Bust Sling Top.
2. For the Flare, put velcro around the waist, hips, and seam.
3. Take the measurements shown in the chart below. The first column is for the vertical length measurements, the second two columns are for the horizontal circumference measurements.

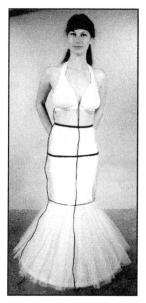 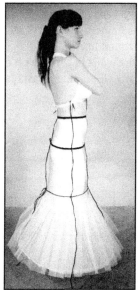 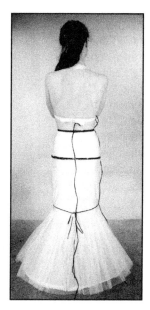

	#	Length	#	CF to Side	#	Side to CB
Rib Cage		0"	10		20	
Waist	1		11		21	
Hips	2		12		22	
Flare	3		13		23	
Floor	4		14		24	

II. Draft the Skirt's Fitted Patterns

This wedding dress requires three patterns for the skirt: one each for the front and back of the skirt's fitted portion; a third for the skirt's Flared portion.

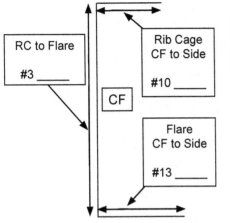

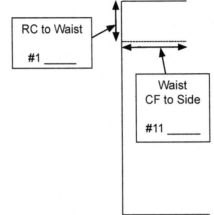

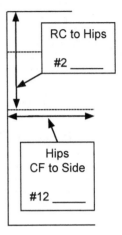

1. Draw a vertical line that is the Rib Cage to Flare seam length #3. This is the Center Front (CF) line.
2. For the rib cage, draw a horizontal line at the top of the Center Front line, then mark off the Rib Cage's CF to Side measurement #10.
3. For the Flare's seam, draw a horizontal line at the bottom of the Center Front line, then mark off the Flare's CF to Side measurement #13.

4. For the waist, measure down from the rib cage line the Waist Length measurement #1, then draw a horizontal line.
5. On the waist line, mark off the Waist's CF to Side measurement #11.

6. For the Hip line, measure down from the rib cage the Hip Length measurement #2, then draw a horizontal line.
7. On the Hip line, mark off the Hip's CF to Side measurement #12.

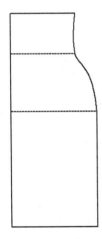

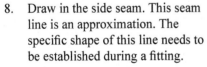

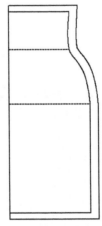

8. Draw in the side seam. This seam line is an approximation. The specific shape of this line needs to be established during a fitting.

9. Add 3/4" (2 cm) seam allowance to the Waist and Flare seams.
10. Add 1" (2.5 cm) seam allowance to the side seam.
11. To create the back pattern on a new sheet of pattern paper, repeat steps 1 through 10.

III. Draft the Skirt's Flared Pattern

Full skirts such as the Flare portion of the Trumpet Skirt can have a fair amount of fullness. The Flare can either be close to the shape of the Petticoat or have additional fullness. In the wedding dress shown, no fullness was added to the top of the Flare. The hem of the Flare is twice the dimension of the Floor measurement.

The Flare for this skirt is a regular cone shape so one pattern can be created then cut several times from the fashion fabric to create two or more gores. The primary consideration is how wide to adjust the pattern for the gore based on the width of the fabric. This width depends on the direction of the knit's maximum stretch which can follow either a fabric's width or length.

Use the form below to calculate how many gores you will need for the Flare. To determine the width of the pattern for the top seam of the gore, use measurements #13 and #23. To determine the width of the pattern at both the top and at the hem, divide the Fullness Desired by the Number of Gores.

Two examples are given: one for 60" (150 cm) fabric with no fullness added to the top of the gore; the other for 45" (114 cm) fabric with double fullness added to the top of the gore.

Note: When performing these calculations, you may end up adjusting the amount of fullness to fit the fabric you are using. Alternatively, you can adjust the position of the pattern when you cut the fabric.

Once you have determined the desired widths for the top and the bottom of the gore, use the instructions on page 154 to create the pattern. The height of the gore will be measurement #4 less measurement #3, page 161.

#	CF to Side	Plus #	Side to CB	Equals	Times 2 = Full Hem	Fullness Desired	Divide by Fabric Width	Number of Gores	Width of Pattern
13	10"	23	10"	20"	40"	40"	–	3	13-1/4"
14	28"	24	22"	50"	100"	200"	60"	3	60"
13	10"	23	10"	20"	40"	80"	–	5	16"
14	28"	24	22"	50"	100"	200"	45"	5	40"
13		23							
14		24							

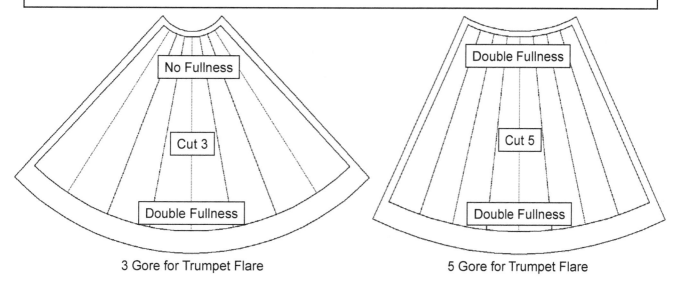

3 Gore for Trumpet Flare   5 Gore for Trumpet Flare

IV. Complete the Wedding Dress

Sew the Bust Sling Top, see page 91.

Sew the Wedding Dress for the Fitting

1. Pin, then use a 4 mm long stitch to sew the fitted body's side seams, right sides together. This stitch length is easier to remove for fitting adjustments.
2. Pin. Then, using a 1 mm zigzag stitch, sew the gores of the Flare, right sides together.
3. Pin the Flare to the fitted body's bottom, then sew with a 1 mm zigzag stitch.
4. Pin, then sew the Bust Sling Top to the top of the skirt, see page 92. This includes sewing the plush elastic to the top of the skirt.

Fitting the Wedding Dress

The only fitting necessary is for adjusting the side seams for an optimum fit and establishing the hem for the Flare.

1. Put the wedding dress on the wearer, wrong side out.
2. Adjust the side seam for an optimum fit.
3. Put the wedding dress on the wearer right side out and establish the hem length.
4. Remove the dress and hem the skirt.

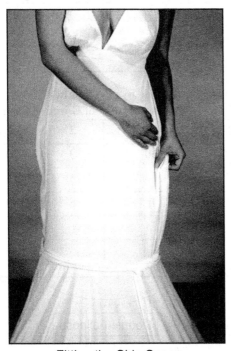

Fitting the Side Seam   Completed Wedding Dress

Appendix

Lingerie Fabric & Basic Terminology
Terminology

Basting – A sewing technique, by hand or machine, that temporarily holds two layers of fabric in place allowing the sewer to focus on the position of the stitching without worrying about the position of the fabric. Basting can also be used to hold elastic in place on fabric.

Denier -- The weight of a knit is measured in denier: 15 denier knit fabric is very lightweight and sheer; 30 is a medium weight knit; 45 is a highly stable knit.

Elastic Allowance – An allowance that establishes the width of the elastic to be sewn in a garment.

Good Side & Wrong Side – Fabric can have two distinct sides: the side that will show on the face of the garment, the "good side," and a side that will be inside the garment, the "wrong side."

Selvedge – The lengthwise edge of woven fabric finished to prevent raveling.

Stretch in Knits – Patterns need to be placed based on the direction of stretch in knits. Some knits stretch across the fabric's width, some along the length, and some in both directions.

- **1-way** stretches in a single direction. An example of 1-way stretch is Satin Lycra.
- **2-way** stretches an uneven amount lengthwise and widthwise. For example, it may stretch 70% lengthwise and 30% widthwise.
- **4-way stretch** has an equal amount of stretch both lengthwise and widthwise. It is used for garments such as leggings, leotards, and swimsuits.

Underlining – Fabric sewn to the wrong side of fashion fabric to add stability. The combined fabrics are then treated as one.

Lingerie Fabric

Lycra and Spandex are one and the same. Spandex is the generic name. Lycra is a name trademarked by DuPont. Lycra can be found in a number of different weights: light (or feather) 2.5 oz to 4.5 oz; medium 5 oz to 6.5 oz; medium heavy 7oz to 8 oz; and heavy 8.5 oz to 10.5 oz.

- **Cotton Lycra** can be used in much the same way as nylon Lycra but is not appropriate for swimwear, which requires fabrics tolerant of chlorine, salt water, and sunshine.
- **Feather Weight Nylon Lycra Lining** is the lightest Lycra at 3.5 to 4.5 oz. It makes excellent lingerie.
- **Heavy Compression Lycra** is a 4-way stretch that has the look and feel of cotton. Excellent for post surgical compression sleeves, leggings, yoga pants, active wear, bras and other foundation garments.
- **Shimmering Lycra** is medium weight nylon with a little sheen on one side and a matte finish on the other.
- **Stretch Satin Lycra** has the look and feel of woven satin and a 1-way stretch.
- **Swimsuit Lycra Lining** is a 4-way stretch lining that has nice body, gives good coverage and does not allow anything to show through.
- **Swimsuit Spandex Lining** is a 2-way stretch Lycra which has a slight brushed surface on one side.
- **Velvet Lycra** has the look and feel of woven velvet but is more durable and easier to sew and care for.

Powernet is a nylon knitted elastic fabric used for control in lingerie such as the backs of conventional bras.

Satinique (satin finish) or **Matinique** (matte finish) are linings for compression type garments such as those for post-operative patients.

Swimsuit & Costume Knit Lining is one of the least expensive types of stretch lining. It is 100% knitted nylon and does not have any Lycra content so even though it stretches nicely, it does not have the resilience of Lycra fabrics.

T-Shirt Knit Lining is 100% knitted cotton lining and does not have any Lycra content. It does have some stretch and is similar to what men's T-Shirts are made from.

Tricot is a warp knit. The fibers run the length of the fabric in a zigzag pattern. Resistant to runs, it is ideal for lingerie and is available in a variety of weights from 15 denier to 60, with 40 being the most popular.

- **Nylon Tricot** (40 denier) can have a shiny or matte finish. It is 100% nylon and is knitted in a manner that allows it to stretch only 1-way (from selvedge to selvedge). Easy to care for and wash, it resists stains and lasts a long time.
- **Sheer Nylon Tricot** (15 Denier) This sheer filmy, gauze-like nylon works well as a sheer lining under lace on bra cups and panties.
- **Stabilized Tricot** is engineered to minimize the stretch inherent in knit fabrics.

Lingerie Elastics

Cotton Swimwear Elastic is approximately 36% neoprene with a 64% cotton covering. It comes in 1/4", 3/8", and 3/4" widths. It is chlorine and salt water resistant for swimwear. Since it has no design element that might cause an itchy feeling, it is good for sensitive skin. Due to the cotton covering, the more it is laundered, the softer it becomes.

Fold-over Elastic is a thin, soft elastic available in 1/2" up to 7/8" wide. It gives a professional finish to the edge of bras and panties. It is folded over the fabric's edge and stitched in place. It is not recommended for swimwear.

Picot Edge Elastic gives a little design element to the edge of garment openings, such as armholes, necklines, leg and waistband openings. Usually it will have a soft feel and sometimes a plush back.

Plush Back Elastic is used most frequently on panties, bras, and other foundation garments, where skin comes in contact with the elastic, such as around the waistband, leg openings, bra straps, band and bra cup areas. It comes in widths from 3/8" to 2". The plush is usually on the back side of the elastic but a few have a light application of plush on both sides.

Rubber band Elastic looks like a greyish white rubber band and is a little thinner than most other elastics. It is not made out of rubber or latex and is chlorine and salt water resistant and suitable for swimwear and is a more economical type of swimwear, or lingerie elastic.

Satin Ribbon Elastic Strap is like a firm satin ribbon that has stretch. It comes in 3/8" and 1/2" widths. It does not have a plush back. It is not as thick as regular strap elastic.

Strap Elastic, in general, is a much stronger, firmer elastic then leg or waistband lingerie elastic and can have a shiny, satin finish or a dull, finish. It comes in a variety of widths: 1/4", 5/16", 3/8", 1/2" 5/8", 3/4" and wider. It gives a lot more support in bras and bustiers. Most strap elastics have a plush back, making them feel kinder next to skin.

Mini-Me Dress Form

These instructions show how to make a Mini-Me Dress Form for the waist to floor region. This form can be used to evaluate a fabric's look for draping and fullness. It can also be used to develop a prototype for an original wedding dress underskirt.

The patterns on the following pages are a Mini-Me Dress Form for the wedding dress model in this book: waist 26" (66 cm), hips 35" (89 cm), waist to floor 40" (101 cm). To change the patterns for a different size body, adjust the hip dimension using the zoom feature when copying the pages. To adjust the waist measurement, change the size of the darts and lines of the side seam. Change the length by adjusting the distance at the knee line during step 4 below.

To make one of these forms, you need 4 sheets of full sheet, adhesive label paper, such as Avery 8165, poster board, and clear tape. Follow the instructions below:

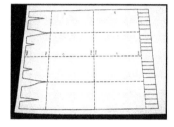 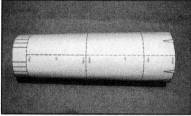 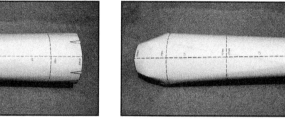

1. Copy page 168 to page 171 onto full sheets of adhesive paper.
2. Cut the pages to remove unnecessary edges.
3. Trim the Waist-to-Knee and Knee-to-Floor forms along the knee line.
4. Apply them to the poster board with the Center Back aligned to the long edge of the poster board.

5. Cut the form along the waist and Center Back lines and at the bottom.
6. To initially shape the form, roll the poster board into a cylinder.
7. Cut the darts and side seams down to the hip level.

8. Tape the darts and side seams closed.
9. Cut the solid slash lines along the bottom of the form. These will become flanges to attach the body of the form to the floor section.
10. Tape the Center Back closed.

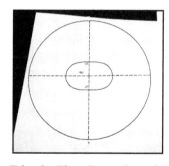 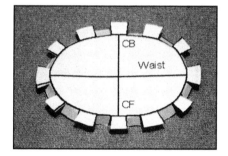 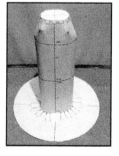

11. Trim the Floor Form along the Center Front/Center Back line, then apply these pieces to the poster board.
12. Apply the Waist Cross Section to the poster board, then cut along the outside circumference.
13. On the Waist Cross Section, clip into each of the slash lines between the two elliptical circles. These are flanges for securing the Waist Cross Section to the body of the form.

14. Starting with one of the flanges just to the side of Center Front, bend every other flange at right angles to the cross section.
15. Put the Waist Cross Section on top of the body of the form. Keep the Center Front flange on the outside of the form, then every other flange on the inside of the form.

16. Tape the Waist Cross Section to the body of the form.
17. At the bottom of the form, bend each of the flanges to the outside.
18. Cut off the flanges marked with an "x." This will aid aligning the form to the Hip Cross Section on the floor.
19. Place the body of the form on top of the floor section, then tape in place.

Waist-to-Knee Form

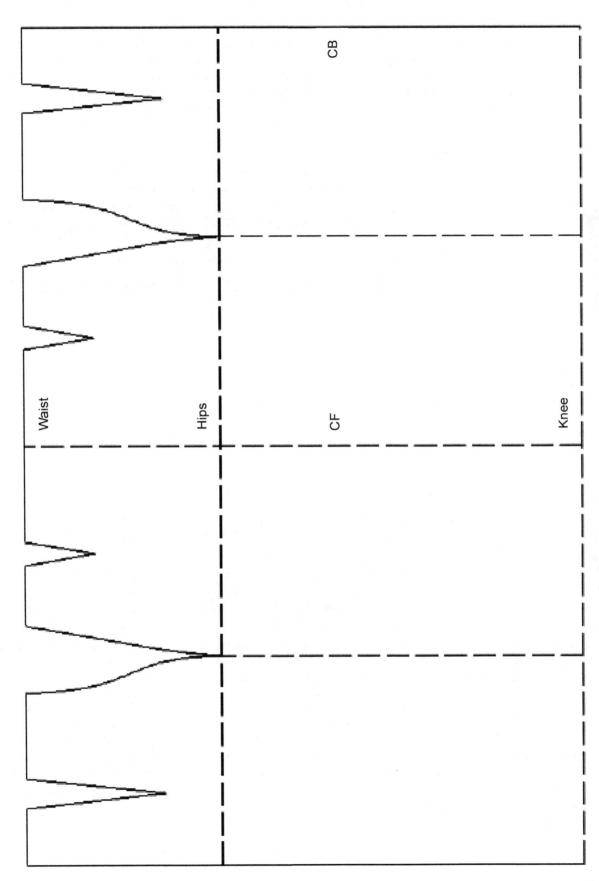

Knee-to-Floor Form

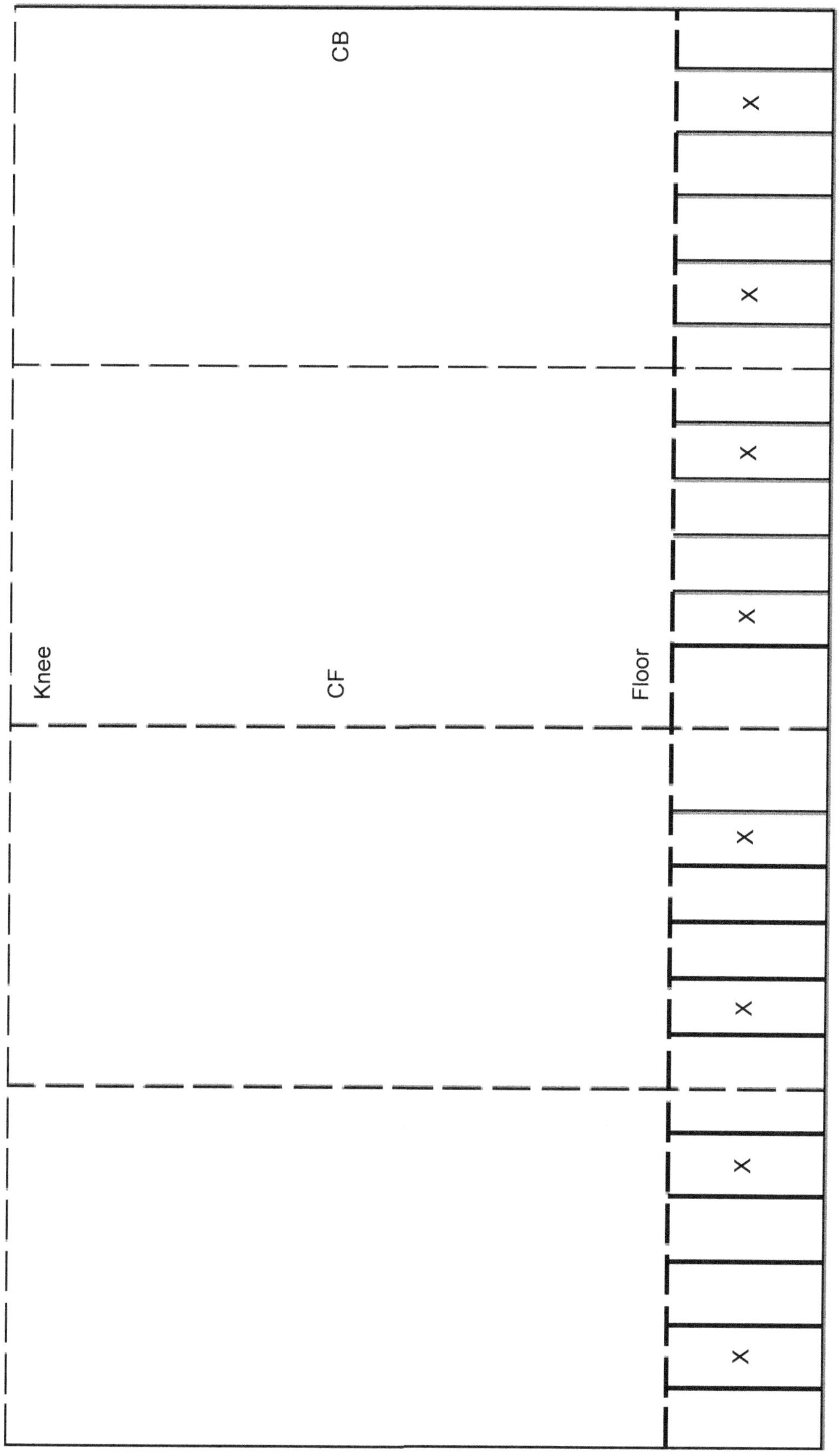

CB

Knee

CF

Floor

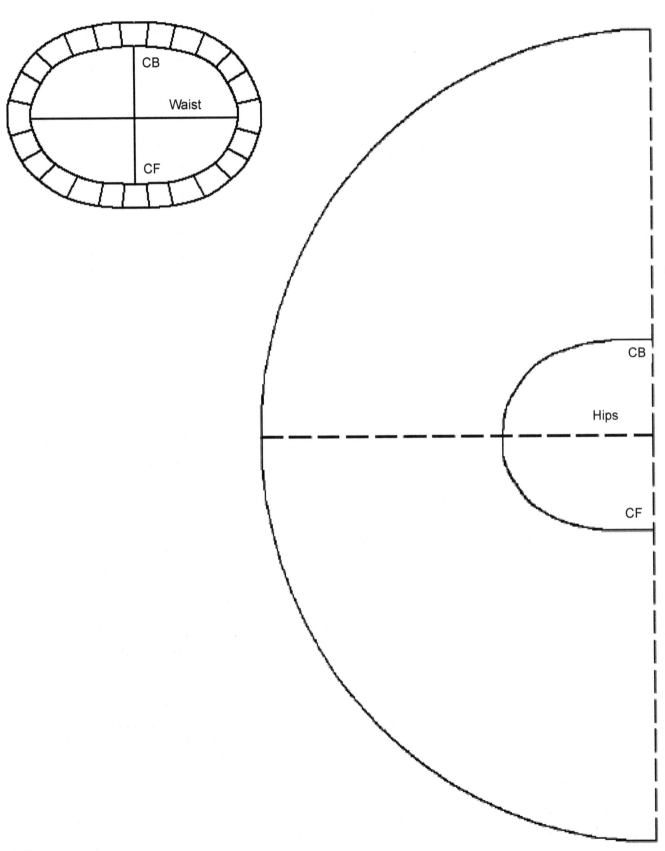

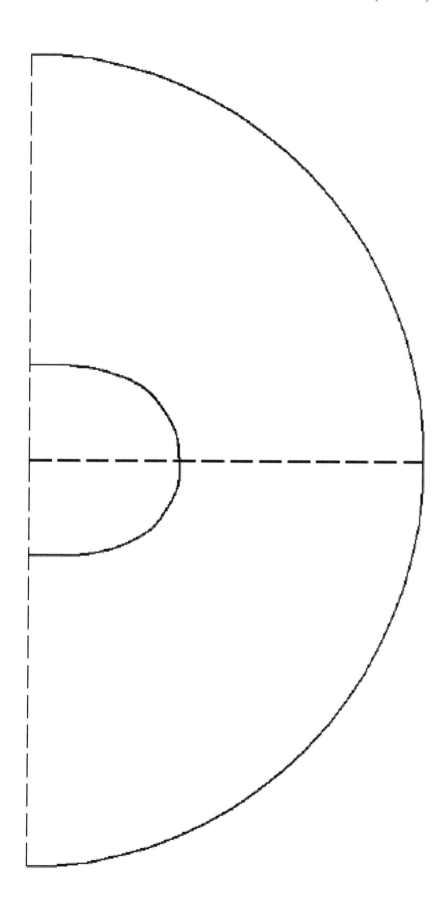

Fabric Testing

The quarter scale Mini-Me Dress Form can be used to determine how a fabric will look in the finished garment. This is surprisingly true despite the smaller scale. To test the fabric, cut a sample skirt that is elliptical for wedding dresses with a train or circular for wedding dresses without a train.

Prepare the Basic Pattern

Patterns for these skirts can be made from the shapes starting on page 173:

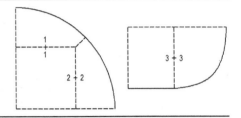

1. Copy these pages onto plain paper.
2. Trim the patterns along the dotted lines that have numbers.
3. Using the numbered notches, tape together the three pieces of the Quarter Circle and the two pieces of the Train Pattern.

Cutting a Circular Skirt

To cut a circular skirt:

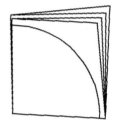

1. Fold the fabrics in fourth as shown in the illustration.
2. Place the Quarter Circle pattern on the fabric.
3. Cut the fabric.
4. On the fabric, mark the location of the center where the Center Front/Center Back line coincide with the side seam.

Cutting an Elliptical Skirt

An elliptical skirt can be used to visualize different train lengths. The chart below shows some of the variations that are possible.

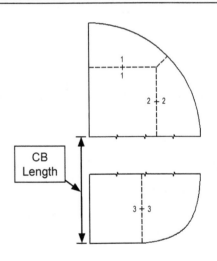

1. On a sheet of pattern paper, trace the Quarter Circle for the Center Front portion of the skirt.
2. Extend the Center Front line down by the CB Length shown in the chart. This length includes the Waist-to-Floor measurement. This is the Center Back line.
3. Put the Train Pattern at the bottom of the Center Back line.
4. Extend the side seam from the front pattern to the back.
5. Place the pattern on the fold of the fabric and cut.
6. On the fabric, mark the location where the Center Front/Center Back line (page 173) coincide with the side seam.

Name	Full Size	CB Length
Brush or Sweep	Just touching floor	11" (2.5 cm)
Court	One foot (30 cm)	13" (33 cm)
Chapel	Five feet (1.1 to 1.5 metres)	15" (38 cm)
Cathedral or Monarch	Eight feet (2.4 metres)	24" (61 cm)
Royal Cathedral	Ten feet (3 metres)	30" (76 cm)

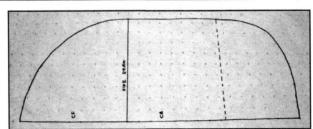

Pattern for Fabric Testing

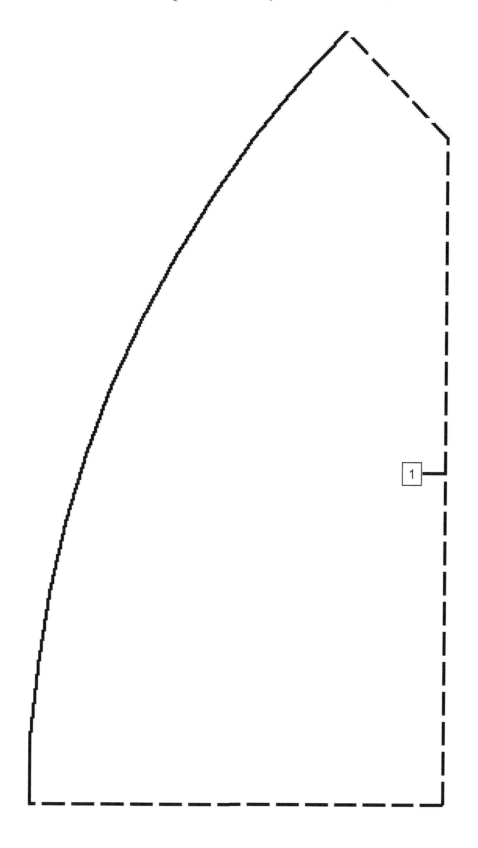

1

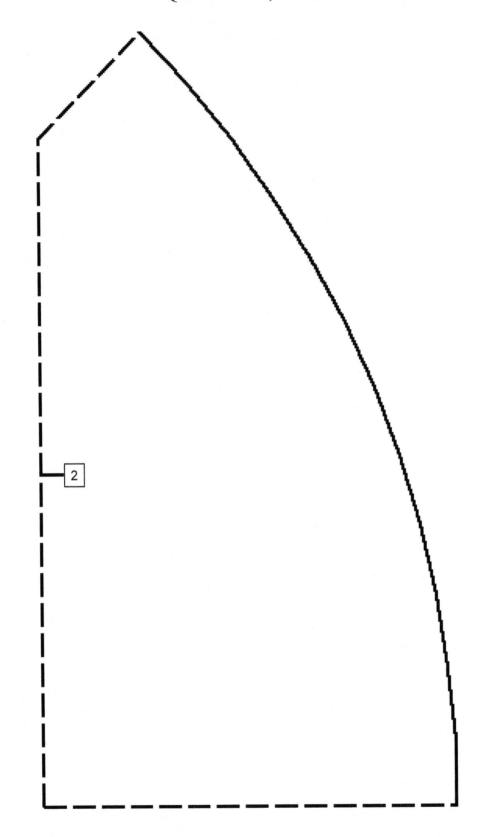

2

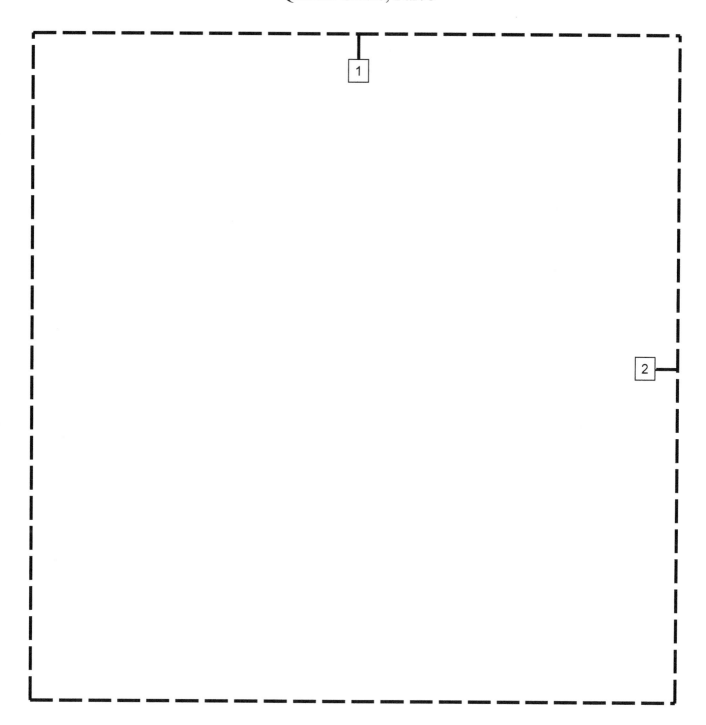

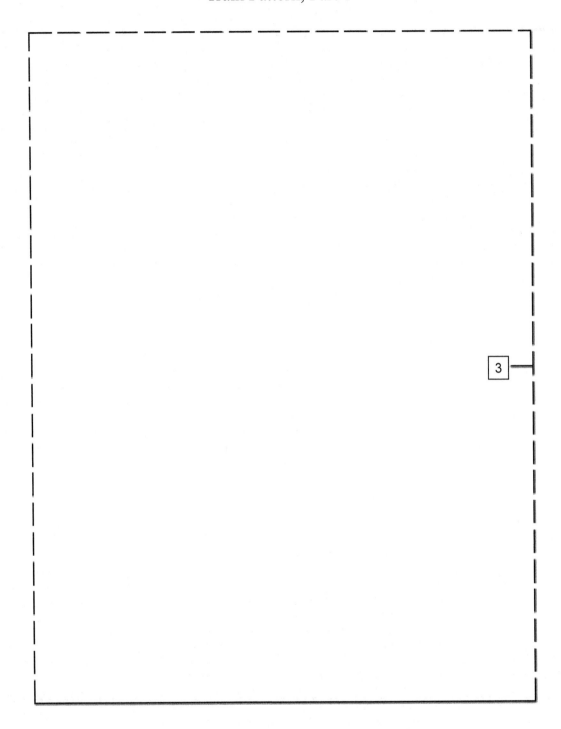

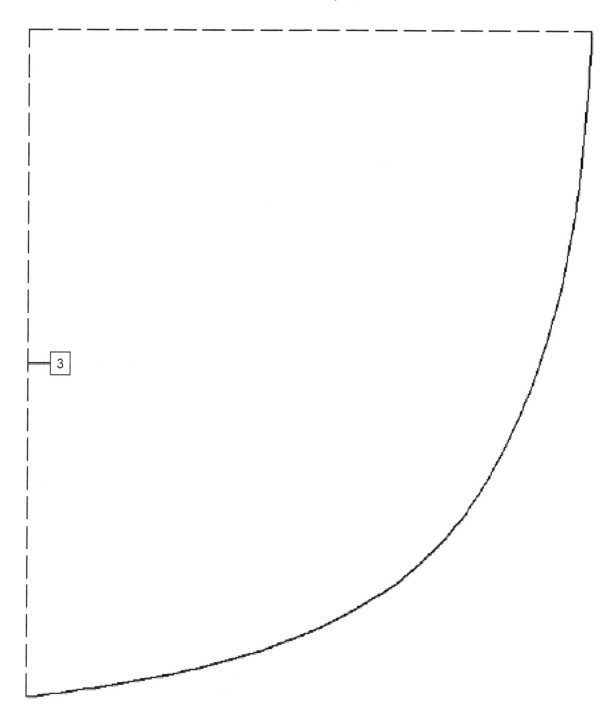

3

Index

CPSIA information can be obtained
at www.ICGtesting.com
Printed in the USA
LVOW05*1544081117
555506LV00018B/274/P